73

We Will Be Shelter: Poems for Survival

ᘓ

Edited by Andrea Gibson

WRITEBLOODY
QUALITY AMERICAN BOOKS

Write Bloody Publishing
America's Independent Press

Austin, TX

WRITEBLOODY.COM

Write Bloody
First Edition
ISBN:9781938912474
Cover art by Ashley Siebels
Proofread by Helen Novielli, Heather Knox, and Andie Flores
Edited by Derrick Brown, Andie Flores, and Heather Knox
Interior layout by Ashley Siebels

Type set in Bergamo from www.theleagueofmoveabletype.com

Printed in Tennessee, USA

Write Bloody Publishing
Austin, TX
Support Independent Presses
writebloody.com

To contact the author, send an email to writebloody@gmail.com

MADE IN THE USA

WE WILL BE SHELTER: POEMS FOR SURVIVAL

WE WILL BE SHELTER

PENDULUM HEART

THEY SAY IT IS NOT ONE THING

AS THE SEA WALKS TOWARDS US

WE WILL BE SHELTER aims to pair helpful poems with helpful causes. Each piece in this book is linked with an organization striving to create positive social change. Our goal it to raise awareness on important issues and encourage the kind of critical self-reflection that inspires a rise to action. We thank the writers and readers of this book for their fierce and compassionate hearts. There is so much work to do. May we do it beautifully.

Royalties from the sales of this book will go to various charities within this book annually.

Andrea Gibson

YOU ARE THE PLACE

LAUREN ZUNIGA

Lauren Zuniga is a queer single mother of two living in the red, red state of Oklahoma. She is the author of *The Smell of Good Mud* from Write Bloody and a three time national slam finalist. Her work has been featured on *Upworthy, Everyday Feminism* and *MoveOn.Org*. Find more poems at LaurenZuniga.com

Third Wave Fund
http://www.thirdwavefund.org

Third Wave Fund is the only national fund that supports and strengthens youth-led gender justice activism—focusing on efforts that advance the political power, well-being, and self determination of communities of color and low-income communities in the US. We partner with institutions and individual donors to invest resources in under-funded regions and social justice youth movements. I chose this organization because they are a community fund led by women of color, trans, and queer folks under the age of 35 and allies.

FEMINISM IS NOT A BRAND OF COMBAT BOOT

We do not check your armpits at the door. It is not
menstrual blood splattered on the lawn of the frat house.
Lesbian man-hating orgies in the back of a Prius.
It is not the awkward Women Studies major with a half-shaved head
and two nose piercings handing you another flier
to the reproductive rights rally. Wait.
Maybe it is that. Maybe it's the way your hairs stand
on the back of your neck, when your professor tells you
you're too pretty to look so angry. Or the one time you stood up
for yourself, they called you a *bitch.* How you squirmed in your
seat as your friends placed bets on which "freshman"
would ruin herself before homecoming.

Maybe it's the outrage when a woman is raped and beaten to
death on a bus in India. The quiet shifting of eyes toward
the countless women, still in the shadows.

Maybe it is the drunk girl at the party. A limp doll carried into
the animal cage. Spat out. Placed on trial.

Feminism does not tell you how to dress. Feminism is the
scandalous girls who wore trousers to the coal mines so you
can wear sweat pants to the grocery store. It is standing
up for your sisters so that your daughters will never be asked,
but what were you wearing?

Feminism is not telling you to stop staying home with your children
and go to work in a bad-ass suit. It is just saying, if you would like
go to work in a bad-ass suit, then BY ALL MEANS, praise our
mothers
& grandmothers and the ally fathers & grandfathers who made
that possible for you.

Feminism isn't a club for straight, white cis-women.
It is not just for women. It's not a political candidate.
But it might be acknowledging that Victoria Woodhull ran
for President of the United States in 1872 and we still have not
elected a woman
as president. We've been trying to get an equal rights amendment
ratified since 1923, meanwhile I still have battle lines drawn across my
body
and my brother will never have to vote for what he can do with his
sperm.
He will make an average of 11K more a year and he will be made fun
of
anytime he cries or acts in anyway feminine
because we all know the only thing worse
than a man being called feminine, is a woman
calling herself a feminist.

- *Lauren Zuniga*

ANNA SHERIDAN GALLAGHER

A former slam poetry coach, thumb-sucker, and semiprofessional couch-surfer, Anna Sheridan Gallagher hails from Oakland, CA by way of Worcester, MA. She's a left-handed middle child who specializes in over-sharing and not doing her laundry. She would like to thank her dad for always writing such beautiful poems for his wife and children.
www.annasheridangallagher.com

It Gets Better Project
http://www.itgetsbetter.org/

Itgetsbetter.com is a storytelling platform where all voices are welcome, a refuge that seeks to remind us of the healing powers of both time and human kindness.

HOLD TIGHT

We are history's unrecorded lovers
Island dwellers, too unnoticed to outlaw
Handcuffed to dishwashers
Born with iron eyelashes pulled
By the magnetic curves of girls allergic to eye contact.
We swallowed the vision
And burnt our tongues.

Subject to the papal logic of men
With cardboard crowns and parachute britches
Us, the gentle rascals,
Lapping birdbaths with our burnt tongues
Our fingerprints left behind on pink petal origami
Who knew being a green-thumbed gardener between bedposts
Would be a political statement?
A practice to be voiced
In order to ink the piles of paperwork that come with validated love.

My friends say I came out of the closet and left the house
Walked down the street and into the moon.
They say I carry a pot of gold around just in case.
I say I'm not sure this country has a mother, just a lot of founding
fathers
(Which sounds pretty gay to me).
But our fathers' children fear fickle mirrors that whisper
"Shh…ame. Shh… aim a bullet
At the target on your Rubik's Cube heart.
Kill that fractured rainbow inside your chest
That will take years to figure out."

For every kid whose heart is sharp-edged and angry
Arms already red picket fences to ward off the wicked,
Hold tight.

Know that fickle mirrors map your freckles backward
So that you will never see you the way I do.

You beautiful owner of busy breath,
You shadow girl with a storm inside,
You bruised soul inside a soapbox,
We need your voice.
You miraculous dance floor of glittering molecules
All those microscopic fireflies
Hold tight.
Magician your mouth
So that black hat vacuum lets loose doves when you speak

Ask for help.
Resist swallowing the key.

The prison guards disguised as monarchy:
King of playground
Of prom
Of pulpit
Of politics
Have not read the fine print of what they preach.
Their mixed textile sweaters
Catching shellfish and pulled pork spittle
Fly in the face of Leviticus
Just like their hardheaded hate.

So ignore the glare of their glass houses
It can blind you sure as sunshine.

Hang your dirty laundry on the line
Like a flag.
Consider it clean.

— *Anna Sheridan Gallagher*

HEIDI ANDREA RESTREPO RHODES

Heidi Andrea Restrepo Rhodes is a Queer, feminist, mixed-race, second-generation Colombian immigrant, writer, scholar, artist, and political activist. Her performance, creative writing, and photography have been seen in places such as San Francisco's SomArts, Galería de la Raza, Harvard's *Queer, Adrienne,* Brown and Proud Press, *Yellow Medicine Review, Nepantla,* the National Queer Arts Festival, and others. She is a passionate advocate for social justice and community healing, and currently lives in Brooklyn.http://heidiarhodes.wix.com/splendormettle

Sylvia Rivera Law Project
www.srlp.org.

Gwen Araujo was just one of the thousands of transgender, transsexual, intersex, and other gender non-conforming people faced with severe and unrelenting discrimination and economic, social, racial, and physical violence due to the social stigmatization and resulting trans-phobia and trans-antagonism toward any person whose body and/or gender expression does not fit within normative notions of the gender binary. Transgender, transsexual, intersex, and gender non-conforming people contend with high rates of unemployment, homelessness, police violence, domestic violence, and hate crimes, as well as impeded access to healthcare, and legal and social services. These are issues that must matter to us all, as true justice cannot afford to leave anyone behind. Among the amazing organizations fighting for rights for these communities is the Sylvia Rivera Law Project (SRLP), "founded on the understanding that gender self-determination is inextricably intertwined with racial, social and economic justice" and "works to guarantee that all people are free to self-determine their gender identity and expression, regardless of income or race, and without facing harassment, discrimination, or violence."

LAMENTATION FOR A BROKEN CONSTELLATION
for Gwen Amber Rose Araujo, 1985-2002

Shovels are for gardening, frying pans
for breakfast & ropes for tug-of-war in the muddy
splendor of summer sunsets. Blankets are for cuddling closely
your friends & darlings in foggy damp sadly-moving winters &
canned food
is for an easy meal when you & your mama have survived another
long day beneath the nail.

They ripped you open to make of your body a kite
that would never fly & the Westboro vultures scavenged
our beat-paused hearts in the name of a stony & callous god,
& I will not forget the clamour & hue of hell in my ear, nor the false
shoe
of panic thrown at the gavel, nor the weeping storm of your bruised
& weary body
clutching to the tapestry, the trance of aspirations & pennies spent
on lipstick & fountain wishes.

I will not forget the fetid fumes of rocky
Masculinities tightening the death lariat against
your trachea & gleam, nor the madness of carrions, those
confused arthropods scratching their heads at your unexpected arrival
to that seat beneath the soil home, nor the surprise of angels
questioning the fist tap
of you & your sidereal sisters knocking early at the liminal door,
mossed twigs in your hair where

flowers should have been, & I will be
loosing the knots at your wrists, ankles, under
the years of these cringing, aching, nightmares, & I will be

grasping at the reddest marigold, ferociously digging the silt of these weathered & fertile flowerbeds, under the empty, mnemonic apertures of a ruddy
& perforated twilight sky.

— *Heidi Andrea Restrepo Rhodes*

GENEVIEVE SAMBROOK

Genevieve Sambrook is a long time introvert/aspiring extrovert living in Southern Vermont. She enjoys writing music, listening to NPR, and the excessive watching of Netflix crime dramas with her brother. Though prone to bouts of prolonged cynicism, Genevieve hopes to make at least one person smile in the next day and a half.

Everyone Is Gay
http://everyoneisgay.com/home/

Everyone Is Gay, founded and run by Kristin Russo and Dannielle Owens-Reid, aims to improve the lives of Lesbian, Gay, Bisexual, Transgender, and Questioning/Queer (LGBTQ) youth through humorous yet deeply moving advice columns, reaching out to Queer youth nationwide, and educating parents. I believe that through Dannielle and Kristin's advice I've begun to accept who I am and where I fall on the many spectrums of gender and sexuality, and can think of no better organization to represent my personal growth in that area.

DAISIES

Wednesday I kissed every inch
of your pulsing neck
and I held your waist
so close to my heart
our breathing matched
you asked me why
I haven't written
a poem in a while
You joked that I was
lacking inspiration
but darling
the heaviest words are so quiet
when something feels right
you just breathe

and so do I

I heard last week on the radio
that for burn victims the only way
to save a limb is to cut it
until it bleeds
so you know where the living starts
every spring my mother has
me slice apart her flowers
she says they grow back
healthier if you remove what has died
darling I've been cutting to
the living part for
as long as I can remember
I would like to think I am
growing back

— *Genevieve Sambrook*

17

SUZY LA FOLLETTE

Suzy La Follette received an MFA in poetry and non-fiction at Antioch University Los Angeles in 2013. She is the founder and editor of *Spoken Word Review* www.spokenwordreview. com, placed sixth in the National Poetry Slam in 2003, and her non-fiction piece, Reading Smoke, was nominated by Antioch to represent the school in AWP's Intro Journal's Project. Her poems have appeared in Spry Literary Journal, Cactus Heart Press and bars across the country. She is a career firefighter, plays bass and sings in a band called Arty Twit and the Alibis www.artytwit.com, and lives in Austin, TX.

Girls Rock Austin
www.girlsrockaustin.org

Ann Richards School for Young Women Leaders
http://www.annrichardsschool.org.

There are two organizations, dear to me, that share the essence of this poem: both Girls Rock Austin and the Ann Richards School for Young Women Leaders. Girls Rock Austin is a summer camp that inspires the same lively independent spirit in young girls that leads them to follow any dream they may have, from shredding the guitar in a band, to fighting fire. Ann Richards School for Young Women Leaders is a public all-girls school in Austin. The school's curriculum focuses on science, technology, engineering and math, leading girls to careers where women are often under-represented. Girls face the epidemic of living on the sidelines, cheering for male musicians, wanting to marry a firefighter, thinking we are not good enough, not strong enough. Let's change that.

FORGOTTEN FIRE

Nothing is gentle for me here. The fire's
heat is brief, occasional. It's their eyes
that burn the back of my neck. I was hired
through the same requirements and I'll rise
through the ranks with the same tests. Yet, somehow
I'll have more. With every alarm I prove
my strength, prove my skill, prove my worth. My brow
furrowed, clothes soaked with sweat. But all my moves
are soon forgotten, disappear like steam
rising from my head, with helmet removed.
Surely, when they tell stories they don't mean
to forget me, but they do. In their truth
it must have been one of the guys, that pulled
that body from the car. Now who's the fool?

— Suzy La Follette

ANA CARVALHO

Ana Carvalho holds a degree in Languages and European Literature by the University of Minho (Portugal), where she teaches at the Department of English and North American Studies, and is currently working on a PhD thesis in the field of Comparative Literature and Queer Studies.

Advocate
www.advocate.com

My interest in exploring queer subjects arises from the lack of possibilities that are given to bodies and identities that do not adhere to the male/female order of society to be represented. To consume and produce artworks in which the queer individual is the agent and/or subject of such work becomes a crucial step towards the acceptance and inclusion of such models that disrupt the current dichotomic matrix of representation and, hopefully provides a place for these in-between categories to be included, in a necessary and urgent unsettlement of the narrow and established construction of the dominant male and heterosexual norm that never allows for the creation of alternative identities.

SEAHORSE

i) The street

The words pierce my ears,
Drawing a little metaphorical blood.
I would prefer a kick in the jaw
A cracked rib, a fat lip, a swollen eye
Any other stone that would break my (back)bone
Instead of his male gaze and foul mouth.

The echoing takes me back to school
'Third grader and already a faggot'
Standing in line to the boys' toilet
Unable to piss sitting down as I wish I could
Holding this piece of hanging meat on my trembling hand
Pointing it in my mind at all the bad words that fall around me.

ii) The bedroom

My father's shoes never fit me,
Their tightness hurt, made me limp.
Now I wear my skirt and shirt uniform like a victory
I pin my medal of honour over my left plastic breast
The water of the aquarium will match the five blue letters:
I whisper 'J-A-N-E-T' several times under my breath
An atheist prayer to remind me of my new name.

I tuck my manliness between my legs,
Turn around in front of the mirror
Checking if I can pass for a different pronoun.
Small droplets of blood are drawn from the razor:
The spots where my beard gets thickest and darkest
Are almost invisible under this mask of foundation.

iii) The aquarium

I catch my reflection on the aquarium's glass,
As I track the seahorse's slow ride with my fat index
How I dislike my large knuckles
The hair that I remove every week
Always finds its way back through my pores
Rattling my travesty to the more attentive foreign eyes.

I have taken company for my journey with the seahorse:
The kid, her face still androgynous with young age,
Her pink dress preparing her to sit cross-legged and play housewife
Points at me, kicks my shin, a little blood is drawn.
I have never been as happy as when her mother scolds her
"Do not disturb the lady."

– Ana Carvalho

CASANDRA FAITH

As a member of Slam Richmond, Casandra Faith helped her team to place 8th at the 2012 National Poetry Slam. She is also a staple and staff member at Virginia's longest running open mic, Tuesday Verses, where she began sharing her work in 2007. Currently, Casandra is a teacher of English and creative writing as well as a print journalist for the United States Army Reserve. For more, visit: www.casandrafaith.com.

Service Women's Action Network
http://servicewomen.org.

We're always declaring a "war" on something. A war on drugs. Terrorism. Hell, caterpillars. On rare occasions, there is actually one occurring. There is an actual war against women—in our public lives, in politics, and in media. In this war, we are objects of sexual slurs—the words always vulgar, always meant to tear down and embarrass. Every woman is aware of it because we've all experienced it. Female services members especially, who, unlike civilians, find themselves in hostile environments in which not only their success, but also their survival, is dependent on obeying leadership and trusting their fellow service members. Their experiences in this war cannot go unacknowledged because they, with pride and pain, charge front and center into some of our most horrific battles... not just occurring outside the wire on foreign land, but at home, against those claiming to be on the same side. For those interested in joining this fight, I welcome you to check out Service Women's Action Network (SWAN). Their mission is to transform military culture by securing equal opportunity and freedom to serve without discrimination, harassment or assault; and to reform veterans' services to ensure high quality health care and benefits for women veterans and their families. The organization seeks to accomplish this mission through policy reform, media advocacy, litigation, and community organizing.

WAR ON WOMEN

September, 2002.
Upon completing basic training, my company commander shared the
following with the females of Bravo Co. 795:
"In this world, you will always be a *bitch* or a *whore*. Decide now which
you prefer they call you."
We'd just learned to maintain and fire M-16s effectively, but we'd not
yet been indoctrinated properly. As women in the Military Police
Corps, we'd be the closest females could ever get to combat.
Her words were preparing us, however, for front lines of a different
kind like...

February, 2003.
I'd not yet mastered tactical maneuvers after dinner and drinks, was
ill-prepared for the blockading of "NO!" from my mouth.
It wasn't a forceful rape.
More like... an apprehensive surrender.
My exposed skin, white flag. A soft target. I became easy prey to a
Staff Sergeant who'd promised he'd square me away.
This would later include $315, a drive to and from an abortion clinic,
and a plea not to tell his wife about what we'd done.

June, 2009.
For refusing a Depo shot strongly suggested to deploying female
soldiers, a fellow squad member accused me of trying to get
pregnant.
As if I had in mind an EPT test's blue plus sign to be my ticket
home, an early trip back from Iraq... as if my choice of birth control
was anybody's business but my own, he stated:
"Well, if bitches can't be trusted to keep their legs closed overseas,
they damn sure can't be trusted to take a pill everyday."
I would later pull convoy security alongside him. Drive. Gun. Work
the same checkpoints he did. Search women and children when he
couldn't, ensuring our safety.
Once home, his wife thanked me for bringing him back in one piece.

Today...
Planted along capitol steps, bills against women lie in wait.
A daisy chain of trip wires.
Rape redefined.
The attempted overturn of Roe v. Wade.
Restrictions on birth control.
Minds set.
Politicians spew, "It is unpatriotic to use the phrase 'War on Women!'"
The phrase somehow disrespectful to the soldiers who've served in a "real war."
Their words, rousing the 144 women who've died while serving in Iraq and Afghanistan... spinning them over in graves and unearthing their sacrifice.
Listen closely.
You will hear a platoon of ghostly voices question:
"What else should we call this then?"
Because war... is a state of hostility. A struggle between opposing forces. A hostile conflict with a particular end.
And this is women against right-winged-Conservative-so-called-Christian-men.
Rush Limbaugh versus sluts and prostitutes, who are to
lay down,
take it,
roll over,
beg
like the good bitches they've trained us to be,
unable to make decisions concerning our own bodies,
yet able to die unacknowledged for this country.

It has always started with a name.
Bitch. Whore.
Feminist.

Terrorist.

And I have fought enough wars to know
labels
that strip us of our humanity

make mass murder

easy.

— Casandra Faith

OLLIE RENEE SCHMINKEY

Ollie Renee Schminkey is a genderqueer poet/activist who is the director of the Macalester Poetry Slam and (as an official Word Sprout collaborator) the founder of Well-Placed Commas, a weekly poetry workshop to serve the needs of the Twin Cities area. They have competed multiple years on nationally ranked Macalester CUPSI teams and Twin Cities NPS teams and are the author of one chapbook, *The Taste of Iron*. They have also performed and published work with 20% Theatre Company's *The Naked I: Insides Out,* and they tour locally with this show, in addition to performing at colleges and other venues across the country. http://ollieschminkey.weebly.com/

RECLAIM
www.reclaim-lgbtyouth.org

When I was caught in a sexually and emotionally abusive relationship my junior year of high school, I had nowhere to go. I was a 17-year-old (closeted) trans kid growing up in a very Catholic small town; I had very few resources available to help me process being raped and abused. I didn't even really have anyone to talk to—but RECLAIM is doing a lot of the work I wish I had access to in high school. RECLAIM focuses on transgender youth in the Twin Cities, creating wider access to integrative health services (mental, physical, and otherwise). They're supporting our trans youth, and that's so incredibly important.

VIRGINITY

My virginity was toddler kissed by Chevy truck,
skull cracked red out onto the pavement. Sixteen years,
a deep voice, the word *bitch,* one laugh and one smile
and too much silence. The way people stare at the impact.
The four hundred dollars I didn't have for the
restraining order. The way he kissed me like a last breath.

With her, now, I can still smell her on my fingers
the morning after. Hers is the first body I've held
that bleeds like mine. I say I don't know what I'm doing.
This isn't what he felt like. What any of them
felt like. Too many men folded over on top of me,
and none of them home like her body.

I tell her I feel uncomfortable taking her virginity.
I say it's not the virginity but the taking.
You will never forget this; even if the road
still faces up clean asphalt. We remember
firsts the way we remember the last.

The last time I went to church, an old priest in a
white robe told me my name
meant rebirth. Renee, the rebirth. But I was not
really born again until I named myself. This *Oliver,*
this steady breath, this strong jaw, this non-binary,
this transgender, this breast and bone, no shame
and finally standing upright. This Other, this queer,
this inconvenient, this loud, this angry. Love.

The last time I wore a dress, they scraped
Oliver off of me, scrubbed clean through to *Renee,*
stuffed my mouth with *woman,* and I have never
been so aware of my thighs. The way my chest
can't sit flat. How small my hands are. How I
am unallowed to occupy my body.

The last time a man touched me, he was every
other man before him. He was splat brain on
a sidewalk, too much muscle. Even though he
wore a different face, he smelled the same. Even
though his hands asked first, he felt the same.

She tells me she doesn't believe in virginity. She
says it casually like there is nothing to take. As if
the body is not a box of cigarettes to be used up. As if
the first time is not a funeral. As if this is a renaming.
And we are the rebirth.

— *Ollie Renee Schminkey*

BLYTHE BAIRD

Blythe Baird is a screen actress, writer, feminist, and hopeful future member of Pussy Riot. In 2014 she was the youngest competitor at the National Poetry Slam, representing Lethal Poetry from Chicago. She is currently a freshman majoring in creative writing and women's studies at Hamline University in St. Paul, MN.

iHollaback
http://www.ihollaback.org/

This organization working to end street harassment is important to me because I cannot remember a time I have ever felt totally safe as a female walking down the road at night. They are combating the power harassers feel by exposing it, striving to create an environment in which we can all share public spaces without feeling threatened. Documenting our stories of being catcalled and harassed have the power to not only change things, but shape policy. iHollaback strives to break the cultural norm of street-side victim silence, inspire international leadership, shift public opinion, and engage elected officials. Supporting women in this fight for safety and independence is crucial.

GIRL CODE 101

We are the finaglers.
The exceptions. The girls
who have not run the mile
in four years

who layer deep V-necks with
excuses. Eyelashes bat wiffle balls
at the male gym teachers.

We are the girls taught to
survive by using our bodies
as Swiss Army knives

calculated scrunched nose giggles
and friendly forearm lingers

You're-so-funny-please-don't-touch-me.

We convince ourselves
there is protection in being
polite. No, you can go first.

Male kindness is so alien to us
we assume it is seduction
every time.

We remember age 9,
the first time we are catcalled.

12, fraudulent bodies
calling us women before we
have the chance to.

13, the year dad says
wearing short skirts in the city
is like driving without a seatbelt.

15, we are the unmarked tardies,
waved detentions, honorable
mentions in lush floral dresses.

16, we are the public
school mannequins.

17, we know the answer,
but do not raise our hands.

Instead, we answer to guidance
counselors who ask us, *Well,*
what were you wearing?

Their voices: clink-less toasts.

We are let off the hook from hall
monitors, retired football coaches
who blow kisses and whisper

Little Miss Lipstick into our
ears in the high school
cafeteria. We shiver,

but hey – at least we still get away
without wearing our student ID's.

This is not female privilege;
this is survival of the prettiest.

We are playing the first game
we learned how to.

We are the asses smacked
by boys who made welcome mats
of our yoga pants.

We are easily startled. Who
wouldn't be?

We are barked at from the street.

We are the girls petrified
of the business school boys
taught to manifest success

by refusing to take no
for an answer.

I wonder what it says about me
that I feel pretty in a dress, but
powerful in a suit.

If misogyny has been coiled
inside of me for so long,

I forget I will not stand
before an impatient judge

with an Adam's apple, hand
grasping gavel, ready

to pound a wooden mark.
Give me a God I can

relate to. Commandments
from a voice
both soft and powerful.

Give me one accomplishment of Mary's
that did not involve her vagina.

Give me decisions,
a wordless wardrobe, an opinion-
less dress.

Give me a city where my body
is not public property.

Once, my friend and I
got catcalled
on Michigan Avenue

and she said *Fuck you*

while I said *Thank you*
like I was trained to.

— *Blythe Baird*

FURY

*** This piece first appeared in *Drunk in a Midnight Choir.* ***
Fury is a despicable changeling creature birthed from the
sulphur swamps of greater New Zealand currently inhabiting
the desolate desert landscapes of Melbourne's CBD. You can
tell them by their webbed fingers and shifting red eyes. To
ward them off, you may leave an inverted coat or open iron
scissors where you sleep however it is not advised to read their
guileful poetry as their words encourage restless sleep. www.
thisisnotapipedream.com

Victorian Aids Council
http://www.vac.org.au/

The Victorian Aids Council is one of the biggest supports
that I've had coming out as non-binary gendered to my family
and dealing with my issues around anxiety and trauma. Solely
catering to queers, it offers a variety of support structures from
HIV testing to counselling services. If you would like to donate,
volunteer or seek help, check out their website at http://www.
vac.org.au/

WORDS WITH FRIENDS

for a long time
my mother and I **didnt**
       a
       l
       k

this is how it is with my family
we are all
tight **lipped**,
     r
     o
     p
     e
     r

dutiful
we swallow
our feelings and they
walk the length of our
throats

in England i **discovered**
      i
      s
      t
      a
      n
      c
      e
works like
a letter opener
tracheotomy

i ducked her calls
preferring radio silence
to following direct orders

the unlikely venue of our reunion
was through the game of scrabble.

As a child,
she would thrash me
unapologetically

i twas
n
f
u
r
i
a
t
i
n
g

just another place she could
chase me
across the board

the last time i played with her
in person
we were in Taupo
three generations of Wilsons
placing tiles like Pompeiian artisans

b
e
l
l
i
g
e
r
a
   n

I held out for **shit**

          then **fuck**

my mother spat my **name**
like an   **x**
             p
    appropriately   four letters long
             e
             t
             i
             v
             e

my grandmother cut her
short

      no
that's a **word**

i was **excused** before I could complete
      u
      n
      t

i refused to play
with my mother again until i got

Words With Friends
on my phone.

it started simply
    at first,
mostly smack talk

but as i started winning,
i gently started
spelling things out

each score
disappearing like evidence

each conversation, too
ironically pitted with her spelling
mistakes
incurred through an apathy towards

s
editing
l
f

when people used to ask her how she
had such well behaved children she would say

I beat them and
lock them in dark cupboards

c

throw her head **back** and

c

k

l

e

her sense of humour was always
so dark
&so off the mark

in our most recent game i told her
her words
you're not gay
had haunted me for

aw

h

i

l

e now

b

l

e

she played the **word**

b

a

I played the **word**

m

off **ivy**

the thing that chokes another to grow itself

other words **pouty**
                um
               p
stocking filler words

things you give when you
don't know what else to do

she tells me now

                              q
i am interested and i accept **you**
              u   **e**
but I just **dont**   **e**
              d   **fear**
              e
              r
              s
              t
              a
              n
              d

her father once threatened to disown her for

                       w
living with her **boyfriend**
out of   **d**
                   l
                   o
                   c
                   k
she told me that

this
h   might be a case of
a
t

a generational
rift
in understanding

i told her to
play
   l
    r
     e
      a
       d
        y

mum,
i said
it's been your move
for days

- Fury

KAREN GRACE

Karen Grace has been an actress, a waitress, a lifeboat captain, a member of the New York City 2013 LouderArts Project Slam Team, and part of the NYC Urbana Slam Committee. Her chapbook, *After Genesis*, was released in 2014 and can be purchased via Tired Hearts Press. Karen currently lives in London with her wife and two kittens where she continues to write poetry and where she desperately misses good New York City bagels. You can follow Karen Grace at gracepoet.tumblr.com or @gracepoet on Twitter

Stonewall Housing
http://www.stonewallhousing.org

Stonewall Housing is the specialist lesbian, gay, bisexual and transgender (LGBT) housing advice and support provider in England. Where many organizations here in the UK neglect to include the Transgender community in their advocacy services, Stonewall Housing provides housing support for all LGBT people in their own homes, supported housing for young LGBT people, as well as free, confidential housing advice for LGBT people of all ages. They also research and lobby for LGBT housing rights, so that all LGBT people can feel safe and secure in their homes, and as a result experience less of the street harassment that is so common for the homeless LGBT community.ek help, check out their website at http://www.vac.org.au/

PRETTY.

It is the first day of summer. I paint my toenails.
I am meeting my girl for dinner and want to look nice.

I am tired of looking disheveled when she sees me,
brush my hair down from the ponytail it stays choked into most days,

add a touch of lipstick. I want to feel pretty.
Not her partner who snores sometimes,

who doesn't always do her part of the housework,
But pretty. The kind she fell in love with first -

that left her imagining what it would be
to kiss the nape of my neck,

or how soft my breasts would feel in her mouth,
or what her tongue would be able to make me do

by instinct and drove her to woo me
in spite of my meanest rebuffs.

And I am the embodiment of this particular pretty
on my walk to the train when it happens -

when the man leaning up against the corner
of the bodega smoking a cigarette

begins walking next to me,
puts his arm around my shadow,

and machetes my silence with:
"I like your pretty toes."

It is not until I am seated on the train,
barreling down through the city towards my love

that I notice my toes:
ten bloody knobs hanging on only by sinews –

the mark of an experienced machete.
They are no longer sexy.

They no longer appear to belong to me.
For a quick fix, I rip off each one.

Do my best to clean them off with a used tissue
found in the bottom of my purse.

I fill the ziplock that earlier housed my lunch with ten painted toes,
stuff it into the pocket of my jeans as far as it will go.

After dinner, I hand my love the baggie.
When she sees the polish on each nail,

her eyes go wide; she thanks me, says 'They're beautiful, honey.'
Says she has something for me, as well, and unzips her hoodie.

Pulling out two bloody breasts, she explains
she didn't have a chance to wrap them.

She hopes I'll be gentle.
They are the most beautiful things I have ever seen.

In bed, we pull out the needle and thread from between the sheets.
Without speaking, she carefully stitches each toe back into position.

When she is finished, she lies on her back and watches my expression
for any hint of displeasure as I suture her breasts back onto her
chest.

When I am done, I cup her face and look into her eyes.
She doesn't miss a beat, says

"You are so pretty."

— *Karen Grace*

SARAH KAY

Sarah Kay has been invited to share her poetry on such diverse stages as the 2011 TED Conference in Long Beach, California; the Malthouse Theater in Melbourne, Australia; and Joe's Pub in New York City, among hundreds of other venues. She has published two books of poetry, *B* (Domino Project, 2011) and *No Matter the Wreckage* (Write Bloody Publishing, 2014). Sarah is the founder of Project VOICE, an organization that brings spoken word poetry to schools and communities around the world. For more, see: www.kaysarahsera.com

Smart Girls at the Party (Change the World by Being Yourself) http://www.amysmartgirls.com

I think this organization is super because it focuses on the "cultivation of the authentic self" and highlights how powerful young women can be. This website provides a positive space for teens, parents, anyone who relates as a smart girl, and anyone who cares for a smart girl.

THE TYPE

Everyone needs a place. It shouldn't be inside of someone else. —*Richard Siken*

If you grow up the type of woman men want to look at,
you can let them look at you.

Do not mistake eyes for hands.
Or windows. Or mirrors.

Let them see what a woman looks like.
They may not have ever seen one before.

If you grow up the type of woman men want to touch,
you can let them touch you.

Sometimes it is not you they are reaching for.
Sometimes it is a bottle. A door. A sandwich.

A Pulitzer. Another woman.
But their hands found you first.

Do not mistake yourself for a guardian.
Or a muse. Or a promise. Or a victim. Or a snack.

You are a woman. Skin and bones. Veins and nerves. Hair and sweat.
You are not made of metaphors. Not apologies. Not excuses.

If you grow up the type of woman men want to hold,
you can let them hold you.

All day they practice keeping their bodies upright—
even after all this evolving, it still feels unnatural,

still pulls tight the muscles, strains the arms and spine.
Only some men want to learn what it feels like to wrap themselves
into a question mark around you, admit they do not have the answers

they thought they would have by now;

some men will want to hold you like The Answer.
You are not the answer.

You are not the problem. You are not the poem
or the punchline or the riddle or the joke.

Woman. If you grow up the type men want to love,
you can let them love you.

Being loved is not the same thing as loving.
When you fall in love, it is discovering the ocean

after years of puddle jumping. It is realizing you have hands.
It is reaching for the tightrope when the crowds have all gone
        home.

Do not spend time wondering if you are the type of woman
men will hurt. If he leaves you with a car-alarm heart,

you may learn to sing along. It is hard to stop loving the ocean.
Even after it has left you gasping, salty.

Forgive yourself for the decisions you have made,
the ones you still call mistakes when you tuck them in at night.

And know this.

Know you are the type of woman
who is looking for a place to call yours.

Let the statues crumble.
You have always been the place.

You are a woman who can build it yourself.
You were born to build.

— *Sarah Kay*

KAYLA WHEELER

Kayla Wheeler is a nurse and feminist writer living in New Hampshire. She is a NorthBEAST Underground Team Slam Champion and has represented Slam Free Or Die at the National Poetry Slam. Her work has appeared in various literary journals including *FreezeRay, Drunk in a Midnight Choir, The Orange Room Review,* and *Wicked Alice.* Follow her at kaylahwheeler.com

Women, Action & the Media
http://www.womenactionmedia.org

Despite the fact that there are 3.3 billion women in the world, they make up only a fraction of the mainstream media's voice. Women, Action & the Media is a North American non-profit whose mission is to foster an environment devoted to gender justice in the media. To learn more about WAM! and to get involved in your local chapter,
please visit: www.womenactionmedia.org or
email:wam@womenactionmedia.org

GROWING UP GIRL IN FOUR PARTS

In November 2013, The Motion Picture Association of America censored a scene in the film Charlie Countryman, in which actress Evan Rachel Wood receives oral sex from her male co-star. The scene was deemed 'too graphic' to be granted an R rating.

I. In junior high, my best friend was named Megan.
She wore spaghetti strap tank tops all year and was
the tallest girl in school. One sweaty afternoon before summer
break, the hockey boys invited Megan and I to the back
of the bus. I slid nervously onto a leather seat next to Megan
who whispered, *we have to make out*. When I asked her why
she said, *I don't know, just do it*. I never tell anyone
Megan was my first kiss, because though I puckered my cherry
chapsticked lips, I knew that kiss did not belong to us.

The next fall, a pigtailed pre-teen left, "how to properly give
a blow job" on the browser of a school computer.
Ms. Hubert, after assuring us we'd no longer be virgins
if we swallowed boys like pints of bad cafeteria milk
said, *better to keep the boyfriend you have than be
used goods to another*. As girls, we are taught to give
before we ever learn what our own bodies are capable of taking.

On the way home from school that day, I bought three bags
of Ring Pops. Wore them only on my ring finger.

II. In the film Saving Private Ryan, blood pours from soldiers' heads
like spilled buckets of paint, bodies are scattered across Omaha
Beach
as if nothing but fresh road kill. In slow motion, Tom Hanks watches
one of his men search the nearby sand for his arm, which just got
blown the fuck off. And to think, that the only thing more offensive
than this blood-soaked mess is watching a woman receive pleasure.

Three minutes of sex that does not also include a man getting off
is too repulsive for a national audience.

III. The Accused. The Last House on the Left. Irreversible. The Girl
with the Dragon Tattoo. The Hills Have Eyes. The Poker House.

All of these films depict violent scenes of rape or sexual assault,
none of which were censored for rating or viewer discretion.
Evan, hasn't Hollywood taught you that the dissection of your body
is more profitable than its willful opening? What a pretty fool
you are to not know they will give you what you want, but
they don't want to see, even if you are obviously faking it.

IV. Katy Perry's 2008 hit single 'I Kissed a Girl'
was number one. For seven weeks.

Megan moved to Vegas years before, but I always thought
that if I heard it from the speakers of her mother's red muscle
car I would have hated it a little less. That maybe,
if Megan and I were on the set of a movie, we could sneak
to our dressing room and hold each other, apologize
for what we didn't know and how it broke us
into becoming women, while the rest of the world sits
and just keeps watching.

— *Kayla Wheeler*

WHAT DO YOU KNOW ABOUT HEAT?

SONYA RENEE TAYLOR

Sonya Renee Taylor is an award winning performance, activist and founder of The Body is Not An Apology an international movement and organization focused on radical self-love and body empowerment. She is the author of A Little Truth on Your Shirt, a collection of poetry and her work appears in numerous journals and anthologies. She tours nationally and international facilitating workshops, speaking and performing. She resides with her Yorkshire terrier in Oakland, CA.

The Dream Defenders
http://dreamdefenders.org/vest/

The Dream Defenders develop the next generation of radical leaders to realize and exercise our independent collective power; building alternative systems and organizing to disrupt the structures that oppress our communities.

WHEN THE SHOTGUN QUESTIONS
THE BLACK BOY

"Darius Simmons was by all accounts a good kid" — Black Youth Project

When the shot gun questioned the boy's heart it asked,
"Nigga child, do you sass your mother?
Did you do your chores last night:
before bed, before being asked, before the mule
that pays the bills got home from 2nd shift?
Are you a good kid?

Where's your daddy Darius? Did you run em off?
Did you cry too much? Eat too much?
Did you weep over your father's footprints?
Did you hold your wilting my mother while she wept?
Did you write him in prison? Did you look for him when he left?
A good kid would have looked for him, Darius.

If you are a good kid, I won't peel your flesh
like the skin of a plum. I won't drill through the oil
of your 13 year old chest boy, if you are a good kid.
A good kid got a jump shot. Nigga you got a jump shot?
You got cash on the light bill? Got something
on that rent this month kid? You got something
 on that rent? You ain't got that trap dough
to buy them kicks you want?
You ain't got no way to help? A good kid would help.
Help but don't hip hop. Don't hug blocks.
Don't get caught hugging other boys,
faggot!
Don't get caught Darius.
A good kid won't wear his pants like our expectations.
Did you were em low Darius?

I swear I'll stop one eighth of an inch
from you sternum if you are a good kid.
If you don't whistle at white women Emmit/Darius.
Don't reach for your wallet Dialllo/Darius!
Don't be getting married in the morning Sean/Darius!
Don't be getting handcuffed on Subways Oscar/Darius!
Don't be looking for help late at night Renisha/Darius
Don't be playing that music all loud Jordan/Darius
Don't be walking dark from a corner store with no bag of skittles
NIGGER!

If you ain't one of those bad ass niggas,
I won't rip through your Sunday service dress shirt.
Make your mama bury you in it.
Won't make your mama watch you drop
like a shell casings kiss. Darius,
we don't let weeds grow round here.
Not those on honor roll or the ones with a nickel
sack of worthless in his book bag. I am sorry Darius.
I am obligated to remind you;
the only good black kid
is a dead one.

- *Sonya Renee Taylor*

KAREN FINNEYFROCK

Karen Finneyfrock is the author of two novels for young adults, *The Sweet Revenge of Celia Door* and *Starbird Murphy and the World Outside* (Viking Children's Books). She is also the author of the poetry collection, *Ceremony for the Choking Ghost* and one of the editors of the poetry anthology *Courage: Daring Poems for Gutsy Girls*, both published by Write Bloody.

National Network for Immigrant and Refugee Rights
http://www.nnirr.org/drupal/

Dream. Rise. Organize. *Celebrate!* I chose The National Network for Immigrant and Refugee Rights (NNIRR) because it is a national organization working for the rights of all immigrants and refugees, regardless of immigration status. NNIRR embraces the fight for social justice beyond the issue of immigration as well through programs like LGBTIQ Outreach & Leadership Development Project.

THE NEWER COLOSSUS

My feet have been wilting in this salt-crusted cement
since the French sent me over on a steamer in pieces.
I am the new Colossus, wonder of the modern world,
a woman standing watch at the gate of power.

The first night I stood here, looking out over the Atlantic
like a marooned sailor, plaster fell from my lips parting
and I said, Give me your tired, your poor, like a woman
would say it, full of trembling mercy, while the rats ran
over my sandals and up my stairwell, I was young then
and hopeful.

I didn't know how Europe and Asia, eventually the Middle
East, would keep pushing their wretched through the bay like
a high tide. I am choking on the words I said about
the huddled masses, they huddle on rafts leaving Cuba and we
turn them back. They huddle in sweltering truck backs crossing
the desert and we arrest them. I heard about a container
ship where three Chinese hopefuls died from lack of oxygen
pretending to be dishrags for our dollar stores. How can we not
have room for them? We still have room for golf courses.

I am America's first liar, forget about George Washington.
My hypocrisy makes me want to plant my dead face in the
waves. The ocean reeks of fish and tourism, my optimist heart
corrodes in the salt wind.

Give me your merchandise, I should say.
Give me your coffee beans. Give me your bananas and
avocados, give me your rice. We turn our farmland into strip
malls, give me things to sell at my strip malls. Give me your
ethnic cuisine, your cheaply made plastics, give me, by
trembling boatload, your Japanese cars. Give me your oil.

Not so I can light my lamp with it, but to drool it
from the thirsty lips of my lawn mowers. Give me your
jealousy, your yearning to crawl inside my hollow bones
and sleep in my skin made of copper. Look,

over there is New York. Doesn't it glow like the cherry
end of a cigarette? Like a Nebula from the blackness
of space out here in the harbor? Wait with me. Watch it
pulse like a hungry lion until morning. I should tell you to
enjoy it from here. You will never be allowed to come in.

JARED PAUL

Jared Paul is writer, performance artist, and community organizer from Providence, RI. His work appears in poetry collections and alternative teaching guides such as Write Bloody's forthcoming *Learn Then Burn* anthology and *UnCommon Core* on Red Beard Press, as well as in the *Providence Journal, Socialist Worker, The Agenda, Motif Magazine*, and more. In January 2014 Jared was a member of the largest protest-related class action settlement in U.S. history, Schiller v. City of New York, which set federal precedent against the NYPD's policy of "Group Probable Cause" as justification for mass arrests.

Democracy Now!
http://www.DemocracyNow.org

The world is fire: the mathematical certainty of environmental disaster if global warming isn't halted, oil spills in the Amazon, leaking nuclear reactors, mass economic injustice, racism, sexism, homophobia, hetero-sexism, hate crime, police violence, drone strikes, prisons for profit, human trafficking, violation of First Nation rights, government spying , and countless other atrocities. We cannot solve these issues without accurate reporting of the facts, let alone convince folks to get involved. Democracy Now! is the most thorough and important news program I know of: independent, commercial free, and 100% accountable.

I believe this program has the ability to change the world and I recommend it to all my readers, to audiences at my shows, and over all my social media channels: www.DemocracyNow.org

THE WOMEN IN MY LIFE

Emma said if it meant we couldn't dance
then their revolution wasn't for us.
She said it for her, but when I read
I knew it was for Us.

Angela wrote that prisons were places
designed to keep people like zoos,
not for justice but for control
or profit; and for both.

Amy said that she was not examining
the exception to the rules
so much as she was focused on
the exception to the *rulers*.

Patricia wrote about the chilly room
without politics or hyperbole.
As creator, as funeral fundraiser
for a young son— about survival.

Mémère said love is enough
and for the most part it was true.
Corin said I'm gonna steal my heart back,
Hot Rock to you.

Rosa told me that those who don't move
do not notice their chains.
Lynne said if it is not where I wish to be
then no one can make me stay.

Sarah-Anne tells me I'm handsome,
says that she's proud.
We shared the same womb at different times,

got matching memories now.

Assata wrote that it is our duty not only
to fight for justice, but to *win*.

Bernadine said we are small
but we do not feel weak.

Paula calls me her miracle
says that my first word was *light*.

I'm not always that smart
but when I am, I look up

and thank the stars for the women in my life.

— Jared Paul

CLINT SMITH

Clint Smith is a teacher, poet, and researcher from New Orleans, Louisiana. He is currently a doctoral student in Education at Harvard University, a National Poetry Slam champion, an Individual World Poetry Slam finalist, and has served a Cultural Ambassador for the US Department of State. He enjoys wool socks, burritos, and pickup soccer – not necessarily all at the same time. www.clintsmithiii.com

Race Forward
http://www.raceforward.org

To be a black man in a country that sees us as the antithesis of her greatness is something we navigate every day of our lives. We live in a country whose history is grounded in rendering us as less than human. The world learns to fear us far before they learn to celebrate us. This is in large part due to the ways black men and boys are portrayed in the media, and how our country is inculcated with myopic images of black masculinity. Race Forward is an organization that works purposefully at the intersection of research, media, and leadership development to promote racial justice and achieve the systematic fair treatment of all people.

VESSELS

We are black boys in America.
We are charred vessels,
vestiges of wood and wonder.
Anchors tethered to our bows.
It is the irony of a ship burning
at sea. Being surrounded by
the very thing that should have

saved us.

- *Clint Smith*

ADELE HAMPTON

Adele Hampton is a storyteller, poet, and lover of mason jars with roots planted in DC by way of upstate New York. She has performed at The John F. Kennedy Center for the Performing Arts and is a Capturing Fire Queer Spoken Word Summit and Slam finalist. She is featured in Flicker and Spark: A Contemporary Queer Anthology of Spoken Word and Poetry and was a member of Washington DC's 2013 Beltway Poetry Slam Team.

The Body is Not an Apology
http://www.thebodyisnotanapology.com

Bedtime Stories for Brown Girls is a poem about the process of becoming at peace with my identity as a biracial lesbian. I think it's important to shed light on what it means to be queer in the context of racial identity and how being silent about the hardships can, oftentimes, do more harm than good. This poem, paired with The Body is Not An Apology's message of unapologetic love and acceptance of one's own identity, seeks to unmute the trauma caused by the journey of discovering self-worth and confidence.

BEDTIME STORIES FOR BROWN GIRLS

When I was little, I used to think that I was stuck in a dream and that I'd wake up as a white girl dancing in a kitchen big enough to hold two steps and swinging hips.

When I was little, my mother warned me that my life as mixed girl would be a hard kind of hustle. One heel on the edge of grandma's primed lawns and blue houses, the other on daddy's street corners where glass blankets the bottom of playground slides.

And I know it's no one's fault that I often think of this skin more costume than home. Constantly straddling minstrel show and white picket-fenced perfection.

For some, the definition of trauma is being forced to ignore the casualties of life's havoc, to live in a constant, deafening silence as we choke back the struggle.

Some days, the only thing I can do is picture myself skinny, with blue eyes like my grandmother, with short brown hair perfectly messed up in that way that lets everyone know I'm super gay and super confident and super fit into this community like that full moon fit perfectly framed in my living room window.

I was taught to be a graceful child, so I struck down my vulnerable because we're never supposed to talk about how difficult it is to be different.

Suburban bred, I was raised white with a siren snared in the back of my mouth, like the lump in my throat was the words *I need help,* I kept choking on myself, constantly tying my tongue around the bed post, silently blood-binding the monsters of my two halves — solitude and the faces I wished looked back at me in the mirror.

One day, I thought I could teach my veins how to breathe in the air of my childhood bathroom, all the while thinking how fucking pathetic I was to be afraid to carve out my own skin. To sever the very thing my ancestors worked so hard to march into permanence.

But, what's your response when, *You're not really black,* is laughed in your face by chosen family, when you're dragged to the mall just to sit in stores that never fit because your breasts and back bones were too broad for Victoria's Secret.

High school can be a trap for an already stretched identity.

What's your response when your skin is too light not to be afraid of black hands running through your hair in the locker room after gym class:

So, *you mixed or somethin'?*

It's funny, how I've always come undone when trying to defend myself, trying to present these brown swatches as proof of history. But quick comebacks never came out quick enough because I never thought anyone would accept my naked.

My voice has become a violent, silent sap covering up the hurt I've harbored for years for not being able to erase my own skin.

Some days, I think the bravest thing a person can do is speak their own melanin into a mirror.

I am the clatter of gay, brown daughter to straight, white mother still trying to find the perfect kitchen to dance in.

And I hope to God there is more in me than a wanting to be someone else.

— *Adele Hampton*

CHEYENNE BLACK

Cheyenne Black lives in the Pacific Northwest where she is at work on a nonfiction project related to El Desierto that braids together the Sonoran desert and an exploration of the childhood she had there, including her experiences of witnessed racism and the effects of harsh immigration policies through the perception of a passionate child. This is her first anthologized poem. http://cheyenneblack.com

No More Deaths
http://nomoredeaths.org

The reasons for attempted migration are myriad and complicated by history, inequitable trade practices, and a ballast of words steeped in problematic complication. It remains that there are hundreds of deaths at the border every year that are inexcusable, unnecessary, and uncalled for. Worse, they are preventable.

No More Deaths, No Más Muertes is a direct aid organization (run entirely by humanitarian volunteers) that offers water, food, basic care, and medical aid to individuals and families who are attempting migration through the southern Arizona desert. The aid workers stand as witnesses to the treatment of migrants and respond in life-saving ways. The increasingly militarized desert zone has pushed migrants further into uninhabited areas and forced remote, risky methods of crossing. In addition to providing water stations, they provide much needed life-saving medical care out of a base camp including assistance in avoiding fatal exposure. No More Deaths additionally offers support to deported migrants in Mexico.

To offer water in the desert is not noble, it is the baseline of humanity. Less is indefensible.

EL DESIERTO

The Sonoran is a place where staying alert means
staying alive. The jumpy Gila Monster is a barn-found saw
blade hidden under your pillow; Coyote calls you to
distraction and hails the Peccary on the night spiked frigid—
that breeder of shivers chasing after an escaping sun.
Hollers from the hands bring the Heelers to work and the
hog in the pit and the smoke and the steam rising up from
the coals in the bottom frying the hairs off its back when
you toss it in means a dinner to feed forty when the alfalfa
come in. The Creosotes snake up your nose and make love
to the ajo from the pit. Skeeters prove the foe and hump out
blood on hair-worn brown skin made strap stout and
thorough with Saguaro scars over the shape of sheep
shearing sinew robust in a rodeo ring taking down the calf.
The kind of dirt that hasn't seen drop or dew since Winterlast
breaks a sound under boots that's more snap than grind
where steps go on top but moisture hides below: afraid of
the way the sun sits too close and crying to learn a love for
heat by way of missing it. Rio the savior of the gabacho;
hurto delivers a living under rifle watch.

– Cheyenne Black

AMY DAVID

Amy David has represented Chicago four times at the National Poetry Slam, most recently as a member of semifinalist team Mental Graffiti in 2013. Her work has appeared in journals including *Word Riot, Foundling Review, Shit Creek Review, Danse Macabre, The Bakery,* and *Alight: the Best Loved Poems of WoWPS 2014.* Her debut full-length collection, *No Body Home,* is due out this fall on Blue Sketch Press, and she can be found at https://www.facebook.com/amydavid1.

The Native American Heritage Association
http://www.naha-inc.org/

The South Dakota Badlands is one area of many in the United States that attracts tourists seeking a wilderness vacation while giving little thought to the indigenous peoples who populate the land. Those on South Dakota's Lakota reservations face significant challenges in the present day, including high rates of unemployment, infant mortality and low life expectancy. The Native American Heritage Association works to improve the lives of these communities.

THE SOUTH DAKOTA BADLANDS
TALK BACK TO ME ON MY SUMMER
VACATION

You claim to be from the middle of nowhere
because you grew up without cable television,
your water came from a well that sometimes
ran yellow, and calls to 911 went unanswered
if the sheriff was out to lunch, but be honest:
you had air conditioning, and a local roller rink
and an hour-and-a-half proximity to Wrigley Field.
City slicker, what do you know about the wild?
This is the stuff of legend: the lands that are bad
to cross. The sun is red wine sour and sharper
than an overlit mirror, sleeps less than the waitress
at the Starlite Truckstop, pulls the sweat out of you
like a fast one. At midday, she erases the last
of the shadow and you regret you let your hair grow
long. Nobody gets used to the temperature, they just
become forgeries. What do you know about heat?
The snakes don't know a sparrow from a finger,
a rat from a toe, your voice is the dinner bell,
your footsteps are a checkered flag. Red and
yellow kill a fellow, the hospital is an hour away.
Your cell phone is useless in these parts.
What is beautiful that isn't dangerous?
Watch your ankles, the path is too smooth
like your hardwood flooring, smooth like your
indoor palms, smooth like your politicians.
City slicker, what do you know about America?
Nothing gets a foothold in this earth, not the pebbles,
not the grass, not the fog that settles in
like your mother-in-law on her holiday visit,
not the Lakota homesteaded out, the Ghost

Dancers circled-up like a carousel, believing
God could be stronger than manifest destiny.
What do you know about crime, about massacre,
about Wounded Knee? The four cannons set out
like the points of a cross, bodies searched
like a parking lot, relocation trains coughing up
steam, a hundred fifty natives dead, medals
of honor as the bounty, this land remembers.
Nothing grows here. Call that erosion.
A week from now, you'll show off pictures
of the gullies, the canyons, the chimney rocks,
say everything in South Dakota was hard.
City slicker, what do you know about the country?

– *Amy David*

RASHIDA MURPHY

Rashida Murphy is a Perth-based writer interested in eccentric characters and obscure sorrows. She has published essays, short fiction and poetry. She expects to complete her novel in December 2014, written as part of a PhD in Writing from Edith Cowan University, Perth, WA.

She blogs at http://rashidawritenow.wordpress.com and has a website http://rashidamurphy.com .

VoiceBox

The organization I have chosen is a not-for-profit organization run entirely by volunteers. VoiceBox supports local poets with a conscience and encourages community involvement.

SKIN

Every time
A check-out clerk denies me
My right to be spoken to courteously
And the waitress at a cafe
In an upmarket suburb forgets to serve me

Every time
A bank teller speaks to me
Slowly and loudly
And my name is considered
Too much trouble to be pronounced correctly

Every time
An old man tells me
To go back to where I came from
And a woman at the supermarket curls her lip
At the green-eyed man who holds my hand

Every time
An academic questions the authenticity
Of my qualifications
And a writer says gently
I'm alright because I speak English properly

Every time
I teach a class on diversity
And a student wants to know
If I believe
In white Australian Christian values

Every time
I walk into a room
Where people talk about reffo Muslim terrorists

And someone says loudly
I don't have a racist bone in my body but –

I wonder
If home is length of residency
Or accident of birth
Choosing to speak
Or silencing my skin

— *Rashida Murphy*

SAM SAX

*** Previously published in [PANK].***
Sam Sax is a fellow at The Michener Center for Writers &
the associate poetry editor for *Bat City Review*. He's the
two time Bay Area Grand Slam Champion & author of
the chapbooks, *A Guide to Undressing Your Monsters*
(Button Poetry, 2014) and, *sad boy / detective* (winner of the
2014 Black River Chapbook Prize). His poems have been
published or are forthcoming from *Boston Review, Hayden's
Ferry Review, The Minnesota Review, The Normal School,
Rattle, Vinyl,* & other journals.

Jewish Voice for Peace
http://jewishvoiceforpeace.org

'Jewish Voice for Peace' opposes anti-Jewish, anti-Muslim, and
anti-Arab bigotry and oppression. JVP seeks an end to the
Israeli occupation of the West Bank, Gaza Strip, and East
Jerusalem; security and self-determination for Israelis and
Palestinians; a just solution for Palestinian refugees based on
principles established in international law; an end to violence
against civilians; and peace and justice for all peoples of the
Middle East'

FOLKTALE

in the beginning od said let there be
god and there was god. in ukraine,
the winters were so cold we told
stories about fire. *the four swordsman on*
their burning horses, their burning swords.
king solomon and his flaming underpants.
and my personal favorite, the *old men*
who gave birth to baked bread. my zedee
told me this story from her creaking
wood body buried   in her
creaking wood chair. goes like this:

there weren't always radiators, sam.
all these shower heads you crank
open like a dragon's wet mouth. you
don't know cold, sam. san francisco
has but one season, it's called *easy.*
even in new york, we watch winter
stamped toward us from our hi-tec
down   coats,   electric   blankets
wrapped around our skulls for head
scarves. in the old country we'd have
to rub our legs together how crickets
sing to find love and this is how we
kept warm. also, this is how we made
love. we kept warm all the time. this
is how your father was born. some
days you'd look out into the cabbage
and see people laid out in great big
heated pyramids, rubbing their legs
against each other, some possessed
orchestra,   a   maggid's   accordion,
a field of rocking chairs.

of course a lot of babies came during that next snow year. so many mouths frozen shut. of course there was much sadness, tears hardening on the face. so the town decided to pass a law stating that when we laid together for warmth, men and women slept separate.

i don't know if you know this sam but when two men make love, they also make bread. the slow yeast and butter, yolks breaking in the hand, sugar poured until it makes you sick, you understand this, i know you do, i've read your poems. and you know the older the man the richer the bread. so hashem rose the body temperature of these men until they all sang like ovens. they labored indoors and birthed perfect loaves. that winter, we ate how kings eat. we feasted on the meat of onions, sliced at the dark bread that tasted like my father's heaven. that bread leavened before our home was leveled by men on burning horses. who took our boys away to feed the furnace of empire.

the moral of this story is that for someone who has no bread, no house, and no love. rubbing against a rich old man aint that bad. i know you know this sam, i've read your poems.

but also, that there are many ways to value labor, to eat   and be eaten by love. there are miracles inside us, you see this in how we are here, sam. how we survived the cold unbroken and became something else entirely, not flame,not match head with countless wood bodies, not fire escape drooling gasoline, but something that rises in the heat.

– *Sam Sax*

TIM STAFFORD

★★★ Previously published in *The Berkeley Poetry Review.* ★★★
Tim Stafford is a poet, speaker, and public school teacher from
Lyons, IL. He is the editor of the Learn Then Burn anthology
series. He performs his work regularly throughout the U.S. and
Europe.

Oklahoma Literary Arts Alliance
http://www.olaa.org

I am supporting the Oklahoma Literary Arts Alliance (OLAA).
OLAA organizes literary events focused on youth empowerment,
and community building throughout the state of Oklahoma.
Through their Poets in the Classroom program and the Louder
Than a Bomb Youth Poetry Slam they are showing teachers the
power of the poetry and storytelling. These are programs that I
wish were around when I was a student and programs which
I find indispensable as a teacher. They continue to expose
students and teachers to different points of view, different
cultures, and allow them to come together and build closer
communities.

FOR THE WHITE TEACHER BEGINNING A CIVIL WAR LESSON WITH BLACK STUDENTS

You will never feel whiter
as if you were carved from ivory and
    dipped in vanilla frosting
while smooth jazz plays in the
    background

You will wear long sleeves
to hide the privilege that seeps from skin
yet your collar will still give you away

You will struggle
You will practice
You will still keep saying "slaves"
 instead of "enslaved people"

You will see a hand raised in the back of
    the class
You will know what they are going to
    ask
 "If you were alive back then, would you
    have slaves?"

You will try to answer
Names like Grimke, Garrison, and
    Brown will spill awkwardly

You will hope they bought it
You will know they haven't
Seeing through you as if you had been
riddled with minie balls

You will feel as if you have taken a
cannonball through the chest

You will try to answer again
Citing immigrant ancestors from Ireland, Poland, Germany
White on top of white on top of white
It is not until you get to your home
many miles from where your students live
that you will realize the only acceptable answer
was "no"

-Tim Stafford

CARLOS ANDRÉS GÓMEZ

Carlos Andrés Gómez is a writer and performer from New York City. A star of HBO's "Def Poetry" and Spike Lee's #1 movie "Inside Man," he is the author of the coming-of-age memoir *Man Up: Reimagining Modern Manhood*, released in 2012 by Gotham Books, an imprint of Penguin.

Seeds of Peace
http://www.SeedsOfPeace.org

Seeds of Peace is an international non-profit organization that is dedicated to creating lasting peace in regions of conflict. Their goal is to fundamentally change the status quo in conflict regions by equipping a new generation with the skills, networks, knowledge, and influence that can move their societies from ongoing hostility to lasting peace. While visiting Palestine last year, I saw the horrors of the Israeli occupation in the West Bank first-hand: the Separation Wall that divides families and imprisons people in their homes, abject poverty, and state-sanctioned apartheid. The work Seeds of Peace is doing is a small but important step in ending the conflict between Israel and Palestine.

CHECKPOINT, BETHLEHEM

She asks if I am from *Here*—points to the ground
beneath her feet, our bus straddling the line between
existing and not. I have just visited the birthplace

of the Jesus she wants me to accept. *He is the way*,
she tells me, says I look Palestinian, then apologizes
and giggles when I am not, laughs full-throated as hijab-

crowned grandmothers and thick eyebrowed fathers
scatter out the doors like glass shards, their chins heavy
with time but eyes still floodlit. *They are not looking for us*,

she says, pointing to the guards. Her cadence is suddenly
Cape Town. I remember a Mercedes framed by the garbage
ash of Khayelitsha, how the wires spiderwebbed the smog

to hijack power from telephone cables. Survival is a magic
trick Midwest missionaries and people like me have never
been forced to learn. The IDF soldier in front of me looks

like he started shaving this morning. The stoic barrel
of his M16 winks shrapnel graffiti at my temple,
adolescent mug scoffing at the blue husk of my passport.

He is a casting mistake—overacting in a made-for-TV
movie about Soweto, 1976, channeling the good ole boy
cop he saw in the documentary on Montgomery in fifth grade.

Despite what the red signs tell me, I am more at home
in the goodbye embrace of Khaled than anywhere
that has called me its own. This man I just met. His grace,

his open-armed grace, it feels like something I have spent

a lifetime in search of. Finally, the IDF soldier returns
the crumpled paper stub that proves I exist while huddled

rows of splintered families drift back on like ghosts,
as my oblivious, Evangelical seatmate asks me if I plan
on going to heaven or hell.

— *Carlos Andrés Gómez*

CHARULATA SINHA

Charulata Sinha is a high school senior and an aspiring poet from San Diego, CA. She is honored to be part of this anthology and beyond excited to be published alongside some of her personal heroes. When she is not writing poetry she can usually be found reading or watching poetry.

National Asian Pacific American Women's Forum
http://www.napawf.org

Growing up as a first generation American woman in a culture that alternately fetishizes and fears my home country is a struggle I have faced largely alone by writing poetry. It is vitally important that Asian women have a platform for discourse and dialogue about the unique difficulties they face, and the National Asian Pacific American Women's Forum provides such a resource. Founded in 1996, the NAPAWF works to empower Asian and Pacific Islander American women by promoting and validating their individual perspectives on immigrant issues. With chapters based in cities across America and events, forums, and summits aimed at enacting positive change, the NAPAWF ensures that no Asian woman need face the struggle to reconcile their cultures alone.

TWELVE STEPS TO BEING AN ALL-AMERICAN TEENAGE GIRL

1. Shut up
Purse your lips so they pout
So they are fleshy and pink
Like salmon curled upwards on teak wood, all shiny
Smile and
Breathe through your nose
There, that's it
Shut up
2. Join a fashion club at school
Learn to do things with fabric and sequins
Your fingers will grip the needles like pencils
This hurts
You have blisters now
But look at those pretty buttons
Make a scarf or something
You have a vagina
So it'll come naturally, in time
3. When you realize
Brown girls are built different
Take extra precautions
Burn your passport
Grease the machinery in your tongue
For staccato vowels
And sharp *hello how are you's*
Bleach your skin
Pray they don't notice
4. Throw away your overalls
Your bug collection your marble Ganesh your papier-mâché rocket
You'll need space for the sequins

5. Find a boy with leather seats
And a bobble head on the dashboard
Let him stick his tongue down your throat
When you're pressed against the cup holder
Swallow hard
Try to picture your paper rocket in the air
Connecting the constellations
You could never get it to fly
6. When they ask you to do an accent
Make them laugh
Throw in a couple cow jokes, a call center joke
Pray they do notice
Realize you work the day shift as
Apple pie ingénue
And only moonlight as exotic
When they show up at your door
Late at night
Lips dry and mouths full of sand
Tongues wagging
For cardamom, and peppercorn, and bay leaf
7. Familiarize yourself with the taste of beer
And the taste of concrete
Soon you'll forget the smell of old books
Soon you'll find that your feet can't ride your old bike
The gears have shifted
And the brakes are sticky
Don't worry
The boy will drive you around
8. Throw your dupatta in the washing machine
Stain it and shrink it
Tell your mother you cannot possibly wear it
You are Irish
This is Ellis Island
This is passage and promise land
Deportation is a ship too rocky for your land legs

They will check your tongue for cholera
Just as you swallow the last grains of
Calcutta soil
Swallow hard, again
Remember your rocket
9. They will tease the kid with the turban
Pretend you don't notice
10. The marigold flowers
Will be offered to you as blessing
Your grandmother will kiss them
And pray for you—a good husband, please
Sexist bullshit, you think
As you wax your skin smooth to the boy's liking
The puja bloom will stick to your bleached palms
And you will scrub and scrub
But for days your fingers will smell
Like sandalwood like turmeric like knotted basmati rice
The boy will ask if you are using a new perfume
You will shake your head, No
He must be imagining things
10. Practice your laugh in front of a mirror
Brown girls don't laugh like that
Certainly not in front of men
But this is America
Giggle in this way
When the boy makes the crack
About the Kama Sutra at a party
Don't try to stretch your feet out in your pigeonhole
Remember that America is liberating you
Remember your feathers are the color of dirt
The ground is logically your rightful place
Giggle again
Dig and dig
Stuff your sandalwood palms in your pockets
Pray they notice the bleach is working

Pray they don't notice the soil under your fingernails
And the blood
From your vermillion roots
Working their way into the light
11. As you walk down the aisle
Wearing a beautiful white dress
To marry the beautiful white man you love
Remember that white
Is the color traditionally worn to Indian funerals
You are death and rebirth
You are lipstick
Kali and voodoo
Brown tribal magic
Blonde hair dye
An American wife
How neatly the pieces of your ivory trousseau fit
Smile at this small trophy
You have won something
You cannot tell what
12. Your skin will start to crack
Rivers of wrinkle, sun spot and age
They'll tell you it's growing pains
Do not believe them
Raid the drugstore
Slap every lotion oil cream onto your unforgiving thighs
Try injections, then surgery
They will object
Do not believe them
You are a woman
An American woman
You do not
Give up
So easy

– *Charulata Sinha*

KRYSTAL VALENTINE

Krystal Valentine was born in 1991 and has lived in Augusta, Georgia her entire life. She began her college career as a biology major but will graduate this winter with a Bachelor's degree in English (with a concentration in creative writing). She believes the written voice is one of Man's greatest instruments and is the self-proclaimed puppy princess (she has four dogs).

National Association for the Advancement of Colored People
http://www.NAACP.org

I have chosen the NAACP as an organization that pertains to the themes of racism and colorism addressed in my poem. The NAACP, established in 1909, is the country's oldest civil right's organization. A few of the organization's objectives include "to achieve equality of rights and eliminate race prejudice among the citizens of the United States...to seek enactment and enforcement of federal, state, and local laws securing civil rights...To inform the public of the adverse effects of racial discrimination and to seek its elimination" (NAACP.org). We do not live in a post-racial nation and in light of recent events it is difficult to say much concerning racial tension has changed since our ancestors protested on Birmingham for justice. Organizations like the NAACP fight for the true equality that so often eludes people of color in the nation.

AMIRI'S REVOLUTION.

you are sweet milk stretched with water &
i am sweet milk stretched with water &
we are the recipe for overcoming
that has eluded

corporate bodies
making upper class white american love
in beds too comfortable to creak their
lack of monotony. so,

if you are not too brown for beautiful &
i am not too brown for beautiful, then
get us war hammers
to smash the quiet cradle of the
tenderly birthed genocide
of the museum exhibit of my grandmother's hips.
the breaking news story that is your father's hands.
the zoo attraction of my hair.

is this not our nappy america?
working single mother romance flirting through
police officer kicked out teeth.
little boy skulls branded with cell numbers.
professional lips stapled shut, bleeding broken spine vernacular.
our names are tiaras with the diamonds torn out. so,

if you are not too poor for beautiful &
i am not too poor for beautiful, then
fingernail dig this gold-thirsty desire
from my chest
until touch burns worse
than an overdue light bill.

until your head forgets the way
our prayers grew overripe peach soft,
realizing our words were dust collecting
in upper class white american god's
answering machine.

– Krystal Valentine

PRIYA KRISHNAN

Priya Krishnan is a senior at the University of Maryland pursuing a double degree in Physiology & Neurobiology and Music. She has been writing since her fingers learned to form letters, though she now uses pens and pencils instead of fat sparkly crayons. She can usually be found outdoors, either running on trails or hammocking with a good book. She is a Lannan Fellow, a winner of the 2014 Sebastian Herbstein Memorial Scholarship, and a resident of the Jiménes-Porter Writers' House.

Split This Rock
http://www.splitthisrock.org

Split This Rock is a non-profit organization dedicated to calling poets to a greater role in public life and fostering a network of activist poets. Building the audience for poetry of provocation and witness from our home in the nation's capital, Split This Rock celebrates poetic diversity and the transformative power of the imagination. Split This Rock aims to bring complex issues that are often ignored to the forefront of society. Its programs include workshops, readings, open mics, youth programming, contests, awards, social justice campaigns and poetry festivals focused on poems of provocation and witness. Split This Rock welcomes both monetary support and volunteer services to help its programs flourish.

Reclamation of the body, and of one's origins, through poetry, is a powerful and cathartic process. I was inspired to begin this process after experiencing the transformative power of poetry as a vital tool for social change at my first Split This Rock festival in 2014. The work of Split This Rock has inspired me not only to discover my own identity through spoken word poetry but also to tackle issues that are untouched, to take on the rewarding role of poet as truth-teller.

DARK MATTER

One day my dad asked me:
Did you know American girls
shave their legs?
I didn't say anything
but after I had finished
chopping up functions
into neat derivatives
I ran looking for him at 2 a.m.
because I had sliced my thumb
open with the razor.
He said I didn't mean like that,
I was just saying it.

One day the mirror shouted:
You could make granny panties
look like a thong.
The quiz on the website said
YOU ARE PEAR-SHAPED CLICK
HERE FOR THINGS THAT MIGHT
LOOK GOOD ON YOU.
The bumps on my hips
forgot not to collide
with the edges of doors
on the way out of rooms.

One day my best friend and I
went to a club.
She was disco-ball,
my hair was towel for all the sweat,
my body absorbed
every pinprick of light
that lanced off the wall
and zinged off her.

I was not
fluorescent.
I was hungry for stars,
gulping light between my jaws
like an overzealous planet.
I asked the bartender
for some coffee,
I wanted to spill it
on my arms
and watch it disappear
without staining.

One day in Boston I
sidestepped thirty-one coffee shops
and peered through the glass
of an Indian food store
because I missed the taste
of MSG-flavored noodles.
The shopkeeper's hands
reminded me of the careful way
my mother separated basil leaves
from each other before putting them
into the simmering pot.
The shopkeeper was dumping
the night jasmine with its drooping flower-heads
from the window into the garbage.
The shopkeeper was looking
in a mirror; she was putting
blue contacts over her pupils;
she saw me staring in the window;
she flipped the OPEN sign to CLOSED;
she poured cream into her hand;
she began to lighten her cheeks.

– *Priya Krishnan*

RICK LUPERT

Rick Lupert has been involved with Los Angeles poetry since 1990. He received Beyond Baroque's 2014 Distinguished Service Award and created the Poetry Super Highway (http://poetrysuperhighway.com/). He's hosted the weekly Cobalt Cafe reading since 1994 and has authored 16 collections of poetry, most recently *The Gettysburg Undress* (Rothco Press), and edited the anthologies *Ekphrastia Gone Wild, A Poet's Haggadah* and *The Night Goes on All Night*.

Pico Union Project
http://www.picounionproject.org/

"Love your neighbor as yourself" is the mission statement of the Pico Union Project. They seek to bring diverse cultures together through song, story, art, food and prayer. My poem *Japanese Day* speaks to this idea of remembering your neighbor. It is easy to spend our time traversing through life, ignoring the needs of other humans, whether they're your next door neighbor, or people who only come to life when tragedies such as the Tsunami in Japan put them on our TV's. By supporting an organization like the Pico Union Project, we are reminding ourselves that every other person matters. When one person has a need, we all have that need; and it's our responsibility as an earth-bound human to do our part to make everyone whole.

JAPANESE DAY

Today at the Japanese American
National Museum, we were served

expensive tea and complained
that the other table had chocolate

dessert instead of the banana walnut
we were brought.

Today in Japan a wave washed a house away
ten thousand times.

— Rick Lupert

MEGAN

I'm Megan, a 21-year-old Filipina-Welsh girl who hails from Hong Kong. I've just graduated from the University of Warwick's English Literature and Creative Writing programme. I'm currently navigating the big scary adult world armed with a pen and a notepad. This is the first time my writing has been published and I'm honoured to be part of such a worthwhile cause alongside such talented poets. https://megcamaya.tumblr.com

Love146
http://love146.org/

I believe that Love146 is an organization worth helping because they understand that the trauma of sexual abuse doesn't disappear once the act ends. They create safe spaces and support systems for victims of the child sex industry in places such as the Philippines, where they aim to help those affected regain their sense of identity and self-love with patience and unending encouragement. If you'd like to help, you can either donate on their website or become a part of their street team to help them raise awareness about the child sex industry.

MESTIZA

I used to think I could peel strands of hair like banana
peels and find the correct colour underneath, that if I
spent enough time swimming the black would leach
right out like laundry.

I thought of myself as a scratch card,
if I scratched my dark skin long enough I'd finally win
something but my doctors won jackpots on payments
for antibacterial creams, for months I slept with my
parents because I clawed at my legs in my sleep.

The kids in my class were shaped differently,
I tried to play tag with them at recess and
sometimes they'd let me, but sometimes
they told me it was for girls who were the right
colour – I came home a lot asking to bleach my hair.

I found out my dad was born blonde but his hair
darkened naturally, he said it was the sun so
I spent a year bike-riding in the balconies of the
downstairs car park, hoping for freckles and high
lights and a seen change to wash over me.

I used to ask him why I had mum's eyes instead of
his green ones, but how are you supposed to break
genetic lotteries down for a kid with second-hand
prejudices and scraped knees?

It took a while for me to see my parents' traces
within me, to see the stencils of my mother's eyes
and the mould of my father's nose, to set aside
plastic surgery fantasies.
It took me too long to realise
I like that my skin tans more easily,

that mom keeps a Filipino Barbie in the display
case in the back of my bedroom, a tiny cultural
victory

to listen to a blue-eyed boy stutter to tell me
how much he liked my eyes, to grin at his radio
static laugh as he pressed white skin against my own.

- Megan

PAULIE LIPMAN

Paulie Lipman is a Jewish/queer/writer/poet/music composer out of Denver, CO. He is perpetually on tour/learning/investigating/self-editing/and of course thinking he's going to finish his novel. He hopes to prove himself wrong and right about many of these things.

The Audre Lorde Project
http://alp.org

The Audre Lorde Project is a Lesbian, Gay, Bisexual, Two Spirit, Trans and Gender Non-Conforming People of Color community organizing center, focusing on the New York City area. Through mobilization, education and capacity-building, they work for community wellness and progressive social and economic justice. Committed to struggling across differences, they seek to responsibly reflect, represent and serve our various communities. I have chosen The ALP to accompany my poem on privilege for they fight for and represent some of the groups hit hardest by the fall out of white privilege and privilege in general.

CAMOUFLAGE

Nothing
will reinforce your idea
of white privilege like
a trip to Texas

Forget the jokes,
the wise cracks about
pick up trucks, inbreeding or secession
Far too often humor
gives ignorance a place
to hide, but
so does Jack Daniels
and Lone Star
and unsubtle 10-year-olds
throwing shade at each other across
a soccer field, the epithets
hidden beneath every
"Good game."

You can try to flinch
Can try to feign surprise
Try "Not me."
Try "color blind"
Try "one sixteenth"
Try "some of my best fr.."
Nah, fuck it
Try "post racial society"
and see if it don't catch
on the frayed noose stuck
in the back of your teeth

This is yours, this
cellular inheritance

It's not the Atlas boulder you
claim to have cast off, but
an unfortunate pedestal
whose thin air height
can hoodwink even the best of us
into revisionists
I know, because
it's mine too

I used to think that
I had the right to deny it
That my blood, cursed since
we were framed for the spear
in the side of a messiah
That my people
hounded out of every inch
of good dirt this earth holds
arrogantly convinced me
our holocaust was the first
and only
that the barbed wire Star of David
lodged in our veins branded us
"Other" and "Entitled"

The blue and white borders I fly
have since bled into the rainbow banner
of the men and women I choose
to bring to bed and so many
"Other" flags flown that
my common red beneath
all of this, has been bleached
into gray

But
I can choose
to show you all that
I can choose to
split the stitching and spill
every bit of bi-polar, queer
little Jew boy man-child
at your feet
Never forgetting that
I have the privilege
of camouflage
I can   pass
Even in Texas

The process of owning this
starts with questions
genuine and concise

Then

try silence
try listening
try shutting up long enough
to hear
try realizing the difference between
appreciating other cultures and
holding them hostage
try more questions
and then
if your own camouflage
tricks ignorant motherfuckers into thinking
you agree with them
try facts
try reason
try educating

try eloquence
try reminding them
of every chain rattled
of every blocked border
every auction block
every internment camp
of every holocaust

Try taking every run together color
underneath your skin
and paint their pedestal
so bright they can no longer deny
that it is there

— Paulie Lipman

PENDULUM HEART

SAM SAX

Sam Sax is a fellow at The Michener Center for Writers & the associate poetry editor for *Bat City Review*. He's the two time Bay Area Grand Slam Champion & author of the chapbooks, *A Guide to Undressing Your Monsters* (Button Poetry, 2014) and, *sad boy / detective* (winner of the 2014 Black River Chapbook Prize). His poems have been published or are forthcoming from *Boston Review, Hayden's Ferry Review, The Minnesota Review, The Normal School, Rattle, Vinyl,* & other journals.

The Audre Lorde Project
http://alp.org

"The Audre Lorde Project is a Lesbian, Gay, Bisexual, Two Spirit, Trans and Gender Non Conforming People of Color center for community organizing, focusing on the New York City area. Through mobilization, education and capacity-building, we work for community wellness and progressive social and economic justice. Committed to struggling across differences, we seek to responsibly reflect, represent and serve our various communities."

PRESCRIPTION POPPIES
following sylvia

16.

perfect, to escape in whiteness.
   under the counter cabinet medicines.
      the body, dreaming only of itself.

what numbness carries its burning
   flashlight through my starless blood?
      what science can bottle a stoned

eucharist? let me lay here another hundred
   years, until each knuckle grows a tiny beard.
      both eyes burrowing into the dark

television, comforted by its darkness.
   let me lay here, mother standing above me
      her face slack as an umbilical chord.

she holds a million tiny white eggs
   inside her, each one a bottled god.
      an orange bottle empty in her palm.

god mother, you're blocking the screen.
   calm mother, i'm dulled by the pharmacy.
      i swallowed ten perfect white eggs.

each one hatched suns in my stomach.
   the children of distilled smoke dragons,
      can't you see them? their ten warm yolks

singing heat to my blood. your first
        grandsons numb as my young body
           slung across the floor.

aren't you amazed at how quiet i lay?
        at how much labor goes into the terminus.
           congratulations!

it's a boy.

26.

careful sam, remember this body
        is your last. already, so many friends
           have damaged their wiring or flooded

entirely. twenty six is the year talented
        people die. thank goodness you've had
           to work at this. sweating over the page

until it became something. equilibrium
        is no high. good, you've stopped profiteering
           off your friend's injuries.

every mouth surgery and broken rib
        was a beacon glittering sex in the distance.
           your salt muscle pulling

you toward sustenance. when your lover
        gifts you a wreath of medicines for your birthday,
           with his brother's sick name etched

into the bottle. *stop.* even when your tongue
        sweats a hungry gutter, know that tongues
                are supposed to water. what alchemy turns

gold leaf to bare trees. it is a war,
        you know, the body pitted against itself.
                the brain refusing to flood

this desiccated blood, unless you pray
        to the appropriate gods. i've knelt for years
                at a time before strange medicine cabinets,

swallowed entire beehives for a single
        drop of honey. after all the opium
                has been burned from the water,

after the smoke clears over this flaming
        apiary of a home, know you will only be left
                with what you were born with.

your breath.
your clean blood.
your green bones.

- Sam Sax

KATIE WIRSING

Katie Wirsing was a member of the 2006 National Slam Poetry Championship team, and the 13th ranked at the Women of the World Poetry Slam. Her work has been featured on college campuses across the country, NPR and the BBC. She also opened for The Miami Gay and Lesbian Film Festival, AquaGirl Queer Women's Festival, as well as being the poetic voice for a national commercial.

PFLAG
http://www.pflag.com

In coming out to my extended family, I was very lucky that they were able to set down their conservative views and love me for the person I am. My grandmother especially has been magical (in her way) at opening her heart to the people I have loved and introduced to my big Catholic family. Not everyone has such an easy transition though, and PFLAG is an incredible organization working to bring together queer people and their families. I work a lot with young folks just coming out, and struggling with this exact issue and I always tell them to find a community that celebrates them for who they are, and wait for their family to (hopefully) fall into place. I'm so grateful there is an organization helping to encourage those shifts in healthy and positive ways.

HOPE CHEST

When the trees fell down
and the lights went out,
an audible breath was held around the city.
Soft as an infant's heartbeat,
heavy as a second chance.

When the rain took a pause
and the lightning became not that bad,
we rode our bikes, free as the day we were born.
Naked from the ground up.
There has always been magic in a storm
even the weatherman didn't see coming.

I am a storm the weatherman did not see coming.

At 28 years old,
I have joined my very first 12-step program.
It's all about realizing yourself as a human being.

The first step is acknowledging that *You Are.*

I am working on it constantly.

The apologies I have yet to make in this life
are to the trees that fell the hardest going down.
My spinal cord has never been great
at weathering the storm.
I am my very own fight-and-flight response system.
I yell real loud while I run.
But I have come around more than once
to this very same place in the forest.

I have broken my own record off its turning track
repeating to myself things I know to be true.

There are ten thousand things
I definitely should have told you.
When I was fifteen, my father sat me down at our kitchen table
with five shots of Wild Turkey, lined up like hey baby on the tongue
of a teenage boy in a suburban basement you knew better than.

It was less punishment than learning opportunity.
But it took the better part of a crying hour to get them all down.

To this day, that is the most drunk I have ever been.
But at fifteen, it is difficult to appreciate such awesome attempts at
parenting.
So out of spite, I refused to allow myself to get sick.

This is why I blame my father
for the way I hold things in.
Communication has never been the key
to my broken hope chest.

I blame my mother for my bleeding
that has nowhere to run.
Some days I feel like a volcano with a plug
stuck in my drain pipe.

I am an excellent listener, terrible at talking back.

I have always found it easiest to hang my dirty laundry in a closet
with the door closed. And a padlock.
I am not good at asking for help.
I am not good at taking a stand.

I am the kind of person who makes lists of things
to tell my therapist.
When I see my therapist, I will list her this:

One.
There are mornings I wake up already crying.
Like the weight was too heavy,
even for my dreams.

Two.
Unworthy is a word that takes up so much space.

Three.
On the days that I believe in God,
life is easier.
On the days I don't,
I am nothing but a poison circling the drain.

Four.
Whatever unholy is,
I have been that.
Whatever holy is,
I am dying to become.

Five.
I imagine when you decide you are enough,
peace is a feeling that finally makes sense.

The last one
I always say as a question.
A hopeful song.

- *Katie Wirsing*

ELAINA M. ELLIS

Elaina M. Ellis is the author of poetry collection *Write About an Empty Birdcage* (Write Bloody Publishing). She holds an MFA in Creative Writing from Antioch University and her poems are published in *Muzzle Magazine*, *Vinyl Poetry*, *Splinter Generation*, and the anthology T*he Better Bombshell*. Elaina is Associate Editor at Copper Canyon Press.

American Foundation for Suicide Prevention
http://www.afsp.org

Staying alive is a social justice issue. American Foundation for Suicide Prevention (AFSP) is the nation's leading organization bringing together people across communities and backgrounds to understand and prevent suicide. I share this organization as a resource because I want you to stay alive, and not just you—I want us to stay alive as communities, as queers, as artists, as people who stand outside of the framed family photo on the mantel. AFSP goes beyond saying "please stay here" or "it gets better"—they do advocacy work to reduce the causes of suicide including inadequate healthcare, homophobic bullying, and isolation. If AFSP doesn't sound like your thing, I recommend curling up with a cup of tea, Kate Bornstein's *Hello Cruel World: 101 Alternatives to Suicide for Teens, Freaks, and Other Outlaws*, and your own brave pen and paper.

REVERSE LULLABY

Good morning. Let's begin someplace easy. Under
this blanket, say. This green blanket. The birds outside
are making their bird songs—sounding diagonal,
nearly vertical in their sharp cut through.
The birds do not sound horizontal. WAKE UP.

I meant to say that softly. Good morning. Let's start
with the radio off. Your shirt on. When I looked up "new"
in the dictionary, it meant itself. "New" derives from a long line
of itself: innovative. Previously unseen. Not old. Just bloomed.
No pressure, but language has been doing this forever. Or, sure,

crawl back inside your sweater. Most dreams grow well
in wool and polyester. You might want to send a postcard
out into the fresh air, so that the trees and your parents
know you miss them. Alright, I was being sarcastic, there.
But listen, Honey. Listen, Self, winter does this every year.

2014 did not invent the urge to hide, or the scent
of dread, or the house that you deem too cold to write in. Last year,
it took you six months to clean out one closet. And then
of course, as now, the crocus was sooner and more purple
than you remembered, and the tulips puckered brightly

at the grocery store, though the yard was still bare.
It's not that anything you did or did not do
encouraged the return of okay — spring being its own thing.
But it's worth noting: the woman who showed up
and asked you to love her: she didn't find you

underground, or hiding in your sweater, and it's not all metaphor.
Breathing in is exactly what we do. *I want so badly to say
the things I've said before*, you sigh. Slice through

what's keeping you. Your sweet father reserved, today,
his cemetery plot. He doesn't intend to go out soon,

and neither do you. Wild thing, you are
your own plot, your own urn. We can practice dying
or we can decide to move through winter. No one knows
how to do this, but don't burn or bury what can be used to build.
Around this time last year, you admitted you don't know

how to do this. Today you saw no less than two dozen bald eagles
in one patch of sky. It's time again to pull your hands out of your
sleeves,
make your tools available for pointing, for gestures
of wonder. WAKE UP. It's spring, 2014. Let's applaud
the fact that you're right here, still living.

— *Elaina M. Ellis*

RONNIE K. STEPHENS

Ronnie K. Stephens leans heavily on his roles as teacher and father for inspiration. His poems often explore vulnerability in its many facets. His first collection, *Universe in the Key of Matryoshka,* is forthcoming from Timber Mouse Publishing. http://www.ronniekstephens.com

Youth Services of Tulsa
http://www.yst.org

I was drawn to this topic because, as a teacher, I am constantly aware of how marginalized mental illness is among teens. Those struggling rarely have resources or a safe outlet for their pain, and many attempt suicide because they don't have support systems to guide them through the worst days.

Youth Services will assist 17,000 young people and their families this year with a wide array of programs in four key areas: Runaway and Homeless Services, Counseling, Delinquency Prevention and Youth Development. Youth Services is a proud Partner Agency of the Tulsa Area United Way.

ON LEARNING THAT EEYORE AND OPTIMUS PRIME SHARE THE SAME VOICE, OR A LOVE LETTER TO MY BI-POLAR STUDENTS

I never meant to turn this room into a big-top tent
but the space between bells has become a spectacular act.
Monday is eleven girls on a high-wire in lock-step. Tuesday
is cannons and homeless boys calling themselves men.
Wednesday is a quiet lunch. Always. Thursday
the beasts take center stage. Don't try to tame them.
Friday comes too quickly. There is too much emptiness
for the vacant lot outside. Too many hours
until the next show rolls into town.
I am not a ring master. Most of this is beyond my control.
The lions run wild in the bellies of abandoned mines.
Tread lightly. They will collapse. They will bury their rage
and turn tricks if they hear you coming.
They have learned the shame of survival.
The dull ache of doing what it takes.
But today, a brutal bruise of a boy told me
that the same throat gave life to Eeyore and Optimus Prime.
What subtle trivia. What brilliant balance.
You tired heart. You alien hero.
Look what you can do with this world and a windpipe.

— *Ronnie K. Stephens*

STEVIE EDWARDS

Stevie Edwards is a poet, editor, and educator. Her first book, *Good Grief*, was released by Write Bloody Publishing in 2012 and subsequently won the Independent Publisher Book Awards Bronze in Poetry and the Devil's Kitchen Reading Award. She is Editor-in-Chief at *Muzzle Magazine*, Acquisitions Editor at YesYes Books, and a Lecturer at Cornell University.

As somebody who has struggled with Bipolar II Disorder and/or Borderline Personality Disorder (it seems to depend upon which psychiatrist you ask) since I was a teenager, I am very invested in shaking off the culture of silence and stigma surrounding mental illness. I'd like taking Prozac because you have depression to be no more shocking than drinking orange juice because you have a cold. Poetry is a great tool for addressing mental illness because it can help those who are also struggling with it to feel less alone and can give those who have not dealt with mental illness an opportunity for empathy. There are poems and poets who have saved my life by being brave enough to write about things I recognized in myself that scared and shamed me; I write continuously to repay that debt.

ODE TO PROZAC

O Serotonin Flood,
if I can only know one god, please
let it be you.
Three fathoms deep in your swishing,
I have loved
a stranger's freckled boy
blowing soap bubbles at a kitten on the sidewalk.
I have loved the animal
batting her mitts at the clear, fragile globes.
I have loved the winter air,
the inclined road, the knocking of a shoulder bag
against my right side.
Oh, I know, it was human and good
to ask the boy the kitten's name
and wave at his mother who was waving
and pretty in her snow coat.
Your absence is always a bad face to show
the world that is tired
of bad faces. Is there a right side
to happiness? It is human
to be ruled by chemical and synapse.
It is good to live
unmolested by the glowering horizon.
I do not want to skulk
through the fluorescent corridors of academia
and forget to love the quiet
pointed bulbs of gladiolas—
the gladiolas that are readying themselves
to be beautiful in August
for all of us. In the photo
of my grandmother in her crisp satin
wedding dress, it is August
and she is grinning over an armload

of gladiolas, and I am glad
they are there for her.
I am glad I was held in those arms,
adored like that.
I want to adore the world,
to drink my ginger tea and grin
at every gentle thing I have known
and will know.

— *Stevie Edwards*

ALESSANDRA NACCARATO

Alessandra Naccarato is a writer, spoken word artist and educator based in Vancouver, BC. A proud mad femme, she is a three-time Canadian National Slam finalist who has toured nationally and internationally speaking about resilience, queer identity and the inheritance of struggle. An MFA candidate in creative writing at the University of British Columbia, her poetry and creative non-fiction have been widely published.
www.alessandranaccarato.com

Mad in America
http://www.madinamerica.com

Too often, others speak for us, about us. They tell us what our condition looks like, what it feels like, and how to heal it. In the pathologization of our lived experience, we are taught not to trust our minds, our emotions, our own truths. But those who live with madness know the most about it. I believe our resilience depends upon sharing our stories of survival, in recognizing the knowledge we have and reclaiming agency over our healing. Mad in America is a resource for those rethinking psychiatric care. Based in principals of self-determination, it connects the voices of those living with madness and experts seeking alternative approaches to treatment. It is a space where we can begin writing a different, collective story of madness. A space where we can finally speak for ourselves.

BREAKING & ENTERING

These are my heirlooms: green eyes,
left-hand dexterity and the story of my father,
who at age thirteen hijacked the laundry mat
with a crow bar and a pillowcase

until the room rang with the rain
of quarters on linoleum.

He took his bounty and hitched
from Sault Saint Marie to Northern Alberta
where he saw the aurora borealis
and dreamt of his mother.

But my father, this young thief,
had already broken his mother's heart
and entered the town's most wanted list.

So he flew further north
like a bird who refuses to listen to instinct,
and was arrested in the Edmonton Library
with a backpack of contraband Kerouac,
TS Eliot shoved down his pants.

The Wasteland his only form of identification.

In lockup, he gave no name, number or next of kin.
If you travel far enough, you forget your first language
and my father no longer knew the word for *home*.

So the police named him John Doe. Thief. Vagrant.
Junkie with a highway of track marks.
Madman who spoke to thin air.
They forgot to add the title *son*. Child searching
for his sanity undone by the inheritance of madness.

You see my father, this young thief
only started to run when voices chased him
though all that left him was a thumb on the highway
to somewhere and an itch for a needle of pleasure.

It was in his bones to run.
It was what his father had done.

And in the calamity of adolescence,
I too packed a suitcase of suicide towards
a dead end of addiction.

But here I am.

I have been broken by voices.
I have entered auroras of madness.
But the difference is that when I ran
my mother chased me.

Through the wasteland of Ontario
in the black ice of winter,
and on a street corner of almost
she caught me by the wrist

and said   *this is not your fault.*

Once sentence can change an inheritance.

These are my heirlooms: green eyes,
left hand dexterity, bipolar disorder
and the ability to forgive.
This is not my fault.

And this is not your fault either, Dad.

— *Alessandra Naccarato*

152

MINDY NETTIFEE

Mindy Nettifee is the writer and performance poet BUST Magazine calls "the linguistic orgasm we've all been waiting for." She is the author of two books of poetry, *Sleepyhead Assassins* (Moon Tide Press) and *Rise of the Trust Fall* (Write Bloody), and an indie-press bestselling collection of essays on writing, *Glitter In The Blood* (Write Bloody). In her over 15 years touring, she has performed for audiences of 2 to 2,000, opened for The Cold War Kids, and taught poetry writing and performance at over 100 schools and universities in the United States and Europe. She currently directs the nonprofit Write Now Poetry Society.

The Trevor Project
http://www.thetrevorproject.org

Wake was born out of a commission by the Craft and Folk Art Museum of Los Angeles for an event celebrating ARTIFACTS OF A LIFE LIVED BY THE LIVING (TO LIVE), an exhibition organized around the theme of art as an organizing principal for sanity, a means of surviving and affirming life. I was reminded that art was, in fact, how I survived my youth; and I was reminded of those that did not survive. This piece describes my grief in the aftermath of a suicide that profoundly devastated me. And though I hope it translates to the many languages of grief and loss that belong to us all, I dedicate it in particular to our LGBTQ youth who are struggling with despair. In spite of recent gains in the fight for equality, the CDC continues to report that they are at increased risk for suicide. The Trevor Project is the leading national organization providing crisis intervention and suicide prevention services to LGBTQ young people. The Trevor Lifeline is free and available 24 hours a day – (866-488-7386) – and anyone can speak with a trained volunteer counselor, anytime. If you are moved to act, please reach out to them; they are dedicated to recruiting qualified volunteers to provide life-saving, life-affirming support to LGBTQ youth.

WAKE

We thought our bodies would become police sirens.
We thought we would become, at least, feral wolves
gnashing flint teeth, scoring earth with savage claws
grown the terrifying size of our grief.
We thought we deserved this much:
our howling to sharpen and split the air into knives.
The stars spilling their bloodlight.
The sky on fire.

No one was prepared for it be, instead, the Year of the Lion,
the year we would learn how to hold very very still.
You try it and see how long you can survive—
holding your head as if it is inside the lion's mouth;
holding your body like it's a suspended pendulum
while the rest of world roars on.
See if you can still blame the ones who leave us

having discovered nothing but last straws.
There are many roads to forgiveness,
and we are so exhausted of our own stiff prayers
we are prepared to try them all.
We practice empathizing with the oceans.
We practice candying words into mantras in our mouths.
We practice picturing our lives happening backwards:

the good black dresses uncrumple from the bedroom floors.
The throats unclench. The dark nights purple and unripen.
The body unpanics, arcs back to the cliff edge at graceful angles.
Wine glasses fill their own bellies with rich burgundy.
Confetti floats up angelically into heavens.
Smoke gathers and twists and blossoms into embers, then flames,
then choreographs into the tinseled edges of papers
pressed with secrets. If we keep watching, we will see
where warning signs are born, where Fate gets off.

If we are patient, we will learn to recognize the whites of its eyes.
The door to the invisible must be visible. Every ending is a beginning.
We will walk this back and forth and back again
until it is a slow dance, until it is a pocket of coins unspent,
until we are prophets drunk on the future. We may not be there
yet, but we have left the yawning cages of our despair.
We have given up on wanting to be whole,
but we are still at large. We're free.

— *Mindy Nettifee*

CRISTIN O'KEEFE APTOWICZ

Cristin O'Keefe Aptowicz is the author of six books of poetry (including Dear Future Boyfriend, Hot Teen Slut, Working Class Represent, Oh, Terrible Youth, Everything is Everything and The Year of No Mistakes) as well as the nonfiction books, Words In Your Face: A Guided Tour Through Twenty Years of the New York City Poetry Slam and Dr. Mutter's Marvels: A True Tale of Intrigue and Innovation at the Dawn of Modern Medicine. Cristin's most recent awards include the ArtsEdge Writer-In-Residency at the University of Pennsylvania (2010-2011), a National Endowment for the Arts Fellowship in Poetry (2011) and the Amy Clampitt Residency (2013).

The National Suicide Prevention Lifeline
http://www.suicidepreventionlifeline.org

"Wild Geese" was inspired by a poem of the same name by Mary Oliver. I was in a troubled place in my life, as were several of my female poet friends, when I read that Mary Oliver poem. It sparked something in me, and this poem — dedicated to those friends—is the result.

WILD GEESE
after Mary Oliver

You don't have to be crushed
under the spokes of your own desire
to be proven worthy enough.

The trophies of your hard work
don't have to appear so freshly on your body.
Your clothes need not be torn.

Every night, you worry a new bird's nest
into your hair. Every night, your dreams
grind you under her boot heel.

Your pendulum heart doesn't need
to swing so hard in either direction.
Nails don't have to be bitten to the nub.

You have to believe that the ground will
materialize under your feet the moment
you step forward. No one can tell you

if it will be rock-gravel, or slick with pain.
No one can travel this road before you do.
It is yours, and it is beautiful because of it.

CYNTHIA FRENCH

Cynthia French received her MFA in Writing from Hamline University. She is currently working on a larger collection of poems and stories that deal with the stigm attached to mental illness. She resides in Seattle, Washington. www.cynthiafrench.com

American Foundation for Suicide Prevention
www.afsp.org/

"I'm not crazy," is a phrase I'm much too familiar with, that I have heard friends and family members spit out in defense of their neglecting help for their mental illness. I hope that someday, saying "I'm feeling crazy," will be as normal as "I have high blood pressure." Until then, we can only do what we're capable of to keep ourselves and our loved ones safe

GUIDE TO SURVIVING YOUR
MOTHER'S SUICIDE ATTEMPT

Be prepared for follow up questions.
People don't let you stop with your mother in the hospital.
They want to know about the prognosis, the illness, the cure.

Be prepared that people can't handle the truth.
You can't go all Colonel Nathan Jessup on them.
This isn't a make believe courtroom
and you aren't Jack Nicholson.

Be prepared to tell the truth
or be prepared to lie.
Hint: Lying is easier.

Give your mom an easy cancer or maybe diabetes.
Something chronic, but not completely debilitating.
You'll need a reason to worry about her for a while.

Brace yourself for the string of tilted heads.
The sighs and soft taps to your left arm.

If you decide to say it outloud,
"My mother tried to kill herself,"
do not make jokes.
I know it helps you,
but this is about them.
Not you. Not her.

The story becomes too normal.
You learn just how much to share.
What to keep to yourself.

Describing the scene in the backyard
like it was an episode of *Cops*
makes it more accessible.

This is not their mother. There is distance.
They've never had her homemade buttercream frosting.
They've never stayed up late with her sharing popcorn
from the special popcorn bowl.
They've never sat on the bed watching her push fabric
through the sewing machine.

Don't describe her eyes
How scared they looked.
How empty and scared.
How dark the skin around them was.
Dark and thin and damaged.
Or her fingers. Her hands.
The way they fidgeted.
The way they pulled at her sweater.
The way they felt as she grabbed your face
turning it in different angles, as if she
was looking at you for the first time.

Don't tell them about the journal.
How she called your father a monster.
This is too personal.
Don't even mention it to your father.
He's already forgotten what he read.

Whatever you decide,
end the conversation
by telling them everything is going to be ok.
Even though it won't.

They need closure.
A reason to not have to call you.
A way out of this whole uncomfortable mess.

— *Cynthia French*

162

DERRICK C. BROWN

DERRICK C. BROWN is the winner of the 2013 Texas Book of The Year award for Poetry. He is a former Paratrooper for the 82nd Airborne and is the president of Write Bloody Publishing. He is the author of five books of poetry and three children's books. The New York Times calls his work, "...a rekindling of faith in the weird, hilarious, shocking, beautiful power of words." He is from Elgin right outside of Austin, TX. www.brownpoetry.com

Stay With Me Here
www.stayherewithme.org

As a former paratrooper, the struggles of the depressed and suicidal have always been close to my guts, especially the heaviness felt by soldiers.Former soldiers coming home should look into using their 'special set of skills' with Team Rubicon. Team Rubicon unites the skills and experiences of military veterans with first responders to rapidly deploy emergency response teams when disasters hit. http://www.team rubiconusa .org/ Also, for those feeling suicidal or depression, soldiers and civilians can look into stayherewithme. org.

INSTEAD OF KILLING YOURSELF

...wait

until
a year from now
where you say,
"Holy God,
I can't believe I was going to kill myself before I etcetera'd...

before I went skinny dipping in Tennessee,
made my own IPA,
tried out for a game show,
rode a camel drunk,
skydived alone,
learned to waltz with clumsy old people,
photographed electric jellyfish,
built a sailboat from all this trash,
taught someone how to read,
etc. etc. etc."

The red washing
down the bathtub
can't change
the color of the sea.

Your red washing
down the bathtub drain
can not change
the color of the sea
at all.

THEY SAY IT IS NOT ONE THING

TARA HARDY

Tara Hardy is the working class, queer, chronically ill, Femme poet who founded Bent, a writing institute for LGBTIQ people in Seattle. She is the author of *Bring Down the Chandeliers*, by Write Bloody Press, a former Seattle Poet Populist, writer in residence at Richard Hugo House, an alumnae of Hedgebrook and holds an MFA from Vermont college. Tara tours as a poet, performer, and teaching artist. To contact her or arrange for a performance, visit www.tarahardy.net.

Restorative Justice for Oakland Youth
http://rjoyoakland.org/restorative-justice/

Disparately impacting youth of color, punitive school discipline and juvenile justice policies activate tragic cycles of youth violence, incarceration, and wasted lives. Founded in 2005, Restorative Justice for Oakland Youth works to interrupt these cycles by promoting institutional shifts toward restorative approaches that actively engage families, communities, and systems to repair harm and prevent re-offending. Having trained and made presentations to more than 1500 key justice, community, school, and philanthropic stakeholders as well as youth in the Oakland metropolitan area, and having significantly influenced policy changes in our schools and juvenile justice system, RJOY has already made headway towards its strategic goal of effectuating a fundamental shift from punitive, zero tolerance approaches to youthful wrong doing that increase harm toward more restorative approaches that heal it.

SOMETHING LIKE FIRE

Survivor: "...but I did it because of the trauma."

Survivor—what a pointed word.
What a something to sharpen and jab
at someone. Survivor—what a blockade
to stand behind. What a shield. What a
corner around which to peek
a gun. Explosive to roll into
a party. "Everything I've said and done
is because I am a Survivor!"
When is the day we become responsible

for ourselves? For the ways our damage spills
over, onto others? I want to join a parade
of: This is What I've Done and This is Where
I Did it and This is to Whom. I want a spotlight
on their scars, not mine. I want to carry
my fault on a platter, like a cake
down a street. With the names
of the people I made into a whom
on top. Until everyone comes out
of their houses into the square
and starts confessing, as if
our future depends on it.
(Because it does.)

I want to meet the ones who made me
a whom on the other edge of town
at the end of their cake parade. I want them
to put down their sharp sticks, empty
their cheeks of explosives, and step out
from behind the barricade. I want them
to pull their whole bodies from around

the corner and say, "Me. I did it."
Without blinking or minimizing.
And then I want them to give me
some cake. The slice with my name
on top. But when I take a second look,
I want it to be their name. I want our names
to be the same.
(Because they are.)

And then I want to hug
about it. I want Survivor to be a name
we stop taking in vain, stop using
as excuse. Here, I'll start: I have raged
and thrown and manipulated and coerced and lied and lied and lied
and lied
and lied. Every single time I have held up
the card "Survivor" as if it is a get out of jail
free ticket. But there are real live names
in my wake. In the sea foam behind
my boat. Can't you see their eyes?
The way they spin in the waves—the whites
and the blues and the browns and the hazels
of them? Those are the people I made
into a whom, people to whom I gave
a card, while showing them exactly how to stand

behind it. Survivor—what a pointed word.
What a shield, an explosive. I want the day
when Survivor means a temporary
state, a place to pass through
but not set up permanent, fenced-in
residence. I want survivor to mean something
like fire of renewal after which grows a forest
with as many trees as human complexities.
I don't always want to stomp my feet

on home plate saying, "That person. Did this.
To me." But neither do I want to stand
on the pitchers mound—hurling forward
what someone else pitched

at me. I've been getting this backwards, thinking
Survivor meant I had to toughen
up instead of melt and maybe offer myself
as something to quench. Something to ease,
to nourish and embolden. Don't get me wrong,
I am mad as Volkswagen full of hornets
about what's been done to me, but that doesn't mean
I want to let my stingers out. Not
only because the world needs all of us
to step into the light. But also because what
a day, what a triumph when Survivor means
—I am—
so much more
than what was done to me.
(Because it does.)

- *Tara Hardy*

MEAGHAN FORD

Meaghan Ford is a writer from New Jersey who fell in love with the big city shit. She was a member of the 2014 Boston Poetry Slam team and a National Poetry Slam semi-finalist. She received her Master of Fine Arts from Emerson College and has been called sassy more times than you, I'm sure.
www.meaghanfordpoetry.com

Uproot
http://havenuproot.com/

If you type "dismantling the patriarchy" in Google, Uproot is the first result. If I knew nothing else, that would have been enough. Uproot is the online component of the Detroit-based center, Haven, who strive for the treatment and promotion of prevention education for sexual assault and domestic violence. When I wrote "Bitch," this is exactly what I was hoping to promote—the sort of education that would not only dismantle the levels of oppression experienced by the women in my piece, but also by the men affected by the environment that raised them. You can volunteer or receive aid from Haven if you're in the Detroit area, donate online, and, as always, strive to be a community member that breaks down gender-based oppression and stops violence and harassment where ever they can.

BITCH

He yells from the car window:
Hey Bitch, why don't you smile?
and I scream back,
Because Bitches do what they want!

Now, they think I'm a funny bitch.
A smart bitch— a smart mouth bitch.
A better watch your mouth bitch.
An I could do something with that mouth bitch.

I have stopped smiling at strangers just because
it is something they believe they deserve. I have stopped
being a silent-bowed-head-walk-faster-little-girl.
So when I walk to that man's window I will say clear
and loud: *Your mother must be so disappointed in you.*

The repulsion on his face— every muscle contorting
in confusion, then embarrassment, then anger.
I know he heard me. I will watch that car
speed away because now I'm a *crazy bitch.*
Not worth the effort.

The first person who called me a bitch
was my mother. I was seven years old
and I'd broken something. The word
unfolded itself from her mouth, an easy knife.
Like she'd learned it young.
Like she knew what I would become.

What lessons did my mother's mouth learn
from the women before her? What words did my
grandmother twist between her ribs with a
pay attention smile? *This is what you are born to.*

Don't you know, if you are a bitch first
there is nothing they can still take from you.
I will not teach you how to be a woman.
But I won't teach you how to be a man either.
You're just going to have to be strong instead.

I think of that man in the car, leaving me in his wake.
His earned shame and the way he looked back knowing
he could not apologize for this. How he is still learning
and I am still learning what this strength means.
How he too must be a son of a bitch.
How we both know where we come from.

— Meaghan Ford

KAREN G

Karen G. is a poet-organizer in the Atlanta GA area as well as nationally for poetry slam. She's hosted Cliterati, a queer friendly open mic and hosted poetry slams for more than a decade.

Charis Books and More & Charis Circle
http://www.charisbooksandmore.com/

My shelter, my home, and source of information on any social justice issue is the oldest feminist independent bookstore in the country, Charis Books & More and their programming board, Charis Circle. I plug into them as the alternative to mainstream places to order books for anyone, anywhere. As a community center, they host everything from yoga and readings to the Urban Sustainability and Wellness Project, which is designed to introduce people to resources promoting sustainability and sufficiency beyond capitalist models.

I wrote my poem as a musing and prayer of relationship to animals and our interaction with them on our shared planet. With news of smaller towns curling under the weight of immigrant worker deportations and the predominance of corporate farms, there is a cycle of oppression utilized to put food on shelves. Food, metaphorically and literally, bring issues to the table of class, labor, immigration, race, corporate capitalism, feminism, health crisis, urban laws enacted on rural populations, sustainability, human rights, animal rights and so much more.

PRAYER FOR DEAD CHICKENS

The packaging said
"free range"

the label said
"cage free"

the sticker said
"grain fed"

and I'm not sure I ever believe it
knowing most farms are part of an industrial
complex.

Dinner chicken,
they will tell us anything
to get us to feel good about ourselves
to buy and spend.
The doctor says I need more protein
so here you are
plastic wrapped
in a bag
on a tray
out of a biodegradable box
in the microwave
on the stove
in the oven
on my plate.

Dear chicken,
forgive.

I have seen the eighteen-wheeler metal
the railroad boxcars of shuttering tin

the concentration camps of chickens
the snow of feathers
on the road
fluttering my windshield.

This is for the stun gunned
the broken beaked
the bloody, hormone infused
the pumped up and pressed.

This is for
unidentifiable bits
ground into soups with noodles
for the cold and sick
because humans can be so ill.

Sorry, regret.

This is for hopes that you—stamped and sealed
politically correct chicken—had squirrels
to protect you
and a drooling fang of dog, fox, coyote
to scare you into hand hammered coops.

A blessing

some of us hold heads and hands
in prayer of thanks
for the long pasture to our tables
the sizzle of battered flesh to crunch
the treasure of it.

You are everywhere,
dear bird muscle,
in stock, in broth
in claw at dim sum.

Apologies

for making you so common
a neutral meat
taking on the clucks
of seasoning.

I pray
for the genocides of you
the plucking, where all those feathers go
may they make pillows
not to dream
of you
or where you came from
or if the labels
are a lie.

– Karen G

CARRIE RUDZINSKI

Named Best Female Poet at her first national poetry competition in 2008, Carrie Rudzinski has since performed her work across the United States, New Zealand, Australia, and India. Ranked 4th in the world at the 2014 Women of the World Poetry Slam and 7th at the 2013 Individual World Poetry Slam, Carrie's work has been published in such collections as *Muzzle, Words Dance, Suspect Press, OnMag, Catalyst, Alight,* and *University of California Press.* Her most recent book, *The Shotgun Speaks,* was published in 2013 and is available on Amazon. www.carrierudzinski.tumblr.com

RAINN
https://www.rainn.org/

Forty percent of victims of sexual assault are under the age of 18. Eighty percent are under the age of 30. So often the statistics and stories of sexual violence are overwhelming and feel as though we might never find the strength to navigate through the storm. It is with the guidance and resources of such organizations as RAINN, the Rape, Abuse, & Incest National Network, that our allies become louder and our own voices clearer. With an easy-to-navigate website, RAINN provides services for victims of sexual violence in addition to information for volunteering, educating your communities, and what is being done to address and combat sexual violence in law making. Consider donating, speaking up, and speaking out.

FOR ADRIEN MENDEZ

who ran over a 14-year-old girl with his car three times
because she refused to have sex with him

You thankless womb
You cockroach heaven
You slippery filth
You maggot holy

My gender does not belong to you.

You coat hanger smile
You only child of want
You vulture of greed
You dark panic

My gender is not an invitation.
My gender is not for your trafficking.

My body is not a flag.
My body is not a surrender.
My body is not to be pillaged.

You bludgeon baptism
You fist praiser
You feral boy
You childhood thief
You pedophile envy
You street corner tongue
You want
You take

What body last refused you?
What lover slapped you first?
What child must you conquer next?
What mouth denied your shake?
Who taught you woman is not human?

Pray for the ones who denied you.
Pray for the first to escape you.
Pray for the last to withhold.
Pray for the ones who could not say No.
Pray for the predators who learn from you.
Pray for your flesh.
Pray for your father.

May your drowning be so simple you forget to fight.
May your hands be sawed off and fed to the night.
May you swallow the nightmares of every sex trafficked child.
May every knife hunger for you.
May you bleed out until you fold.
May your choke hearken her bite.
May God forgive you before we find you.

My body is an escape route.
My body knows how to raise the children.
My body is consent.
My body is a wolf pack.
My body bleeds out and is reborn.
My body will devour you right back.

A body just like mine
carried your life inside of it –

But you do not own the body.
You do not get to conquer here.

Human is not for sale,
Human is not for sale,
Human is NOT for sale.

– *Carrie Rudzinski*

DANIEL MCGINN

Daniel McGinn's work has appeared numerous anthologies and publications and his full length collection of poems, *1000 Black Umbrellas*, was released by Write Bloody Publishing. He and his wife, poet Lori McGinn, are natives of Southern California. They have three children, six grandchildren, two parakeets and a very good dog. www.daniel-mcginn.com

Justice for Children Fund
http://www.justiceforchildrenfund.org

The world needs to start talking about a child's rights, adding it to the human rights discourse. Children are stilled owned by their parents and caretakers who are allowed to do so much harm without any recourse. Many perpetrators walk, likely the majority, as our standard of proof is at the highest realm: "beyond a reasonable doubt," and very hard to reach.

Get educated at www.justiceforchildrenfund.org, and make a donation. Or look up the children's advocacy center in your area. There are 600 accredited children's advocacy centers in the US and they cannot survive without community support. They do more for children then could otherwise be possible through the regular system of child abuse response.

THE MEMORIAL

Here's the punch line. Everyone knows.
No one talks about it but you,
you never stop talking.
You and all your words
add up to exactly nothing.

You said a mouthful and then you were slapped.
You were beaten by a woman, keep your big mouth shut.

You don't do grief well—
anger is a part of it.
You don't do anything right
and that makes you angry.

You can't bring yourself to lie, can you?
You stand onstage
at your mother's funeral and ask,
Who were you people, anyway?

It's uncomfortable
this willingness to speak
with a choke on your throat.
Uncomfortable feels like home to you.

Afterwards no one makes eye contact
except a couple of misfits
who shake your hand with their scarred wrists.
The big girl says, *I love you.*
The guy in a dress with mascara running down his cheeks
looks right into you and says, *I know exactly how you feel.*

— Daniel McGinn

SARAH D. LAWSON

Sarah D. Lawson is the founder and slam master of the Beltway Poetry Slam in Washington, DC and a teaching artist through PoetryNOW, an after-school poetry program. She has been a coach for DC's Louder Than A Bomb for the past three years, teaching at The Madeira School, an all-girls boarding school in the DC area. She loves hugs.

Collective Action for Safe Spaces
http://www.collectiveactiondc.org/

Like many women, my body is on display and up for debate and ridicule as I walk through the streets of my beautiful city. Collective Action for Safe Spaces is an organization comprisedof people of all genders who believe in building communities where everyone feels comfortable, safe and respected. Though based in DC, their approach and programs are universal to anyone looking for resources against street harassment.

A CURSE FOR THE CAT CALLERS

The day the snakes take back
your tongues will be the day
you will know the choke
hold of turning corners,
the clench of prayer
in teeth when begging
your own body
to become invisible.

That day you will relearn your thighs
as four course meal,
your shoulders, a plate
for any stranger's tongue to lick clean,
a porcelain bowl on the back wall
of the pawn shop, waiting
to be tagged and auctioned off.

Even then
your body
may still feel
like your own body.

Until they chew
entrance wounds
into your cheekbones.

Until you feel the slobbering
breath of unhinged
when they offer their sex to you.

Until your ass becomes appendage
and you wonder when you shed
into a borrowed thing.

Until *beautiful* feels insulting,
strangers: combat.
the sidewalk, a swamp

of forged permission slips
where everything with eyes
comes to feast.

– Sarah D. Lawson

KYLE JAMES PARKER

My name is Kyle James Parker. I'm 28 and live in a Buddhist Monastery. I spend time writing, speaking and engaging with people about human empathy, with a specialized focus on LGBT humanity. I also tend our garden where I've learned about how maintaining the health of the earth is the key to healthy plants and food. http://kjparker.tumblr.com/

StoryCorps

http://www.storycorps.org

StoryCorps is an independent nonprofit whose mission is to provide people of all backgrounds and beliefs with the opportunity to record, share, and preserve the stories of our lives. We do this to remind one another of our shared humanity, strengthen and build the connections between people, teach the value of listening, and weave into the fabric of our culture the understanding that every life matters.

To have the foundation to make a positive impact in our world we must ground ourselves by listening. We have to know who we are impacting, and we must hear their stories and honor them with our actions. If we only act based on our singular view of the world how can we expect to find harmony? StoryCorps reminds us of the prized art of listening and how to return to our shared bond of humanity.

CITY OF JOY

I've watched victims
Turn into tyrants, their
wounds bleed with wrath.

Holes in the wall become
omens of
forgotten pain I cradle.

The shame of weakness
grows to crack my bones
And now I'm called
the words I've railed against
the nameless hate
a virus that
turns me against myself each time I fear
the daggers in a stranger's eyes.

Has staring into flames
burning to be known seared my eyes
that I am blind to the wounds of the world around me?

Have shrieks of "faggot" deafened my ears
To prayers for freedom from
glass ceilings and iron chains
That rob us of our dignity?

Have I lost my truth
in my desperation to end this pain
that now I have forgotten how
numbness feeds this foe?

Hate
Blinds me,
I

am lost in its illusion
forgetting
my stories are not excuses
but calls to vigilance
to know living truth
to tend all pain,
that I might be thrown open
by life
to be an open door,
a refuge in the storm.

I can listen
I can be the dignity of my wholeness.

My blood will nourish the ground
To grow understanding, not fear.
My ribs will be a gate, open that
each life may enter.
My heart will blaze as a torch
To guide and warm the weary.
My life will be a shelter from oppression
where lovers etch their names
into my mended bones
memorials of living,
testimonies of hope,
stories to teach us how to listen once more
that we can each be
a lighthouse to each other,
a city of joy in the night.

– Kyle James Parker

LAUREN ELMA FRAMENT

Lauren Elma Frament is a poet about to begin her undergrad in mortuary science. She likes Tchaikovsky & going to punk shows. Her work can be found in *nin journal, Drunk in a Midnight Choir, & Borderline Poetry Journal*. She currently lives in New England, but longs for the West Coast.

Girls Rock Camp Alliance
http://girlsrockcampalliance.org/

The first place I ever felt truly home was in my room listening to punk/hardcore. The first time I went to a show, I felt so uncomfortable and unwelcome. I was so angry about everything and I was so angry people were telling me I didn't belong here unless I was straight, white, and had a dick. All the shows I went to in the mid-2000s were dude-fests. Everything, from the lyrics to the banter between songs to the atmosphere in the venue, was misogynist, slut-shaming, lazy, and unchallenging. The scene has since come miles from that, but still has a long, long way to go—most shows I've been to now still consist of mostly dudes, but I see more grrrls opening up the pit and stage-diving and grabbing the mic. There still aren't enough bands who aren't all men. When I found out about Girls Rock Camp Alliance, I was totally stoked—this is a summer camp designed to unite and empower young grrrls through music. This camp teaches the world that gender is not a deciding factor for playing music—you do not have to have a penis to pick up a guitar or form a band or belong to a scene that is, at its core, about unity and love and acceptance in the face of a narrow-minded world.

WILSON STREET, 9:53 PM (THE ACACIA STRAIN SUCKS/BABY'S FIRST PUNK SHOW, AGE 14)

"While sexism hurts women most intimately, it also damages men severely."
—Kathleen Hanna

I am the new girl in a sea of bodies. a boy
grabs the back of my t-shirt, drags me out
of the moshpit by the scruff of it. he is wearing
a hoodie that says, *I HOPE THEY LEAVE YOU TO DIE.*
we are outside Rocko's & this boy is kissing distance
from my face, screaming, *NO CLIT IN THE PIT.*
I want to punch him in his stupid mouth, knock out his teeth,
& I do. my eyes become a post he is tied to, my fists
full of rocks. he looks at me, his face frightened & abandoned
as I imagine it had to have been before he found punk.
I walk back inside, the shitty local bands barreling
into my eardrums, elbow my way into the pit, throwing my limbs
like the most loving stoning.

around here, you have to let your body go among the others—
a wave thrashing against other waves & no one knows
where the shoreline is. around here, if the mic gets passed to you,
you yell along even if you don't know the words. around here,

   bruises mean you're in the family, & in this family,
   if someone hits you, you hit them back.

— *Lauren Elma Frament*

SHELBY HANDLER

Shelby Handler is a Seattle-based queer Jewish poet, organizer and teaching artist. Rooted in a tradition of diasporic tongues and loud mouths, they have been writing and performing poetry since the age of fifteen. Shelby coordinates Youth Speaks Seattle, the city's premier youth spoken word collective. Follow them @shelbyhandler.

Powerful Voices
http://www.powerfulvoices.org/

Patriarchy is a powerful system of oppression embedded in each layer of our society. From the interpersonal to systemic and institutional levels, sexism intersects and interlocks with other oppressions: racism, classism, heteronormativity, ableism and more. Holding the complexity of these issues, the Seattle-based organization Powerful Voices bravely imagines a world where "all girls live healthy and personally meaningful lives in a society that values them." Through education, employment, community building and case management programs, Powerful Voices invites young women to vision a more just world where they get to show up in all of their identities and all their power.

THE BITCH'S BELATED ODE
for the boys I grew up with and the men they're becoming

The boys love a lie
and an ashtray.
The boys lick the soot
off each other's dicks.

The boys have never been the ocean.
The boys have always been
the salt
on the rim
of an asshole.

The boys are petaled
fools, folded up on themselves
like a library of spit.

The boys are seeing you
and you should turn
as pink as the corsage.

The boys are breaking
the wine glasses again.
The boys kiss
like empty cupboards.

The boys hollow you out
and make you confess.
You, the *slut* and the *bitch*,
the knife they wanted to pocket
at the end of the night.

You, the sharp
and the easy sheath.
You, that thing to be filled.

The boys call the cunt *a sewer,*
a swamp, an axe wound.
The boys just joking.

They wouldn't say it to her face.
The boys just will be boys.
But the boys not like other boys.
The boys are nice guys.

The boys get so tired of being nice,
really, the boys don't see it paying off yet.
The boys don't see the wolf in their own jaws,
the boys do not see the tool
in their own sheds.

The boys do not check the gender box marked 'weapon'.
As far as they know.
They swear they don't.

They swear they love their mothers
and aren't nauseous at the thought of the blood
she can draw without lifting a finger.

The boys did not forget
how they been clipped
like buds from a wombed tree.
The boys did not mean to mistranslate.

The boys did not mean to lean
all their fire into your face,
Didn't mean to spill the ash on your lap,
or foist the booze on your chest.
The boys did not hear your joke.

Say it again.
Say it again
for the teeth.

The boys made you *pretty*
by naming you that.

Flowers weren't flowers
til a man gave them that noose.

The boys didn't buy you dinner,
the boys bought you.

- *Shelby Handler*

MCKENDY FILS-AIME

Mckendy Fils-Aime hails from Manchester, NH. He is the author of three self published books of poetry. Some of Mckendy's work can be found or is forthcoming in *Amoskeag, Radius, decomP*, and *FreezeRay*. The only thing he likes as much as poetry is his sneaker collection.

Division of Children, Youth & Families
http://www.dhhs.state.nh.us/dcyf/

The Division of Children, Youth & Families plays an instrumental role in maintaining the health and wellness of families throughout the state of New Hampshire. Over the years, it has established itself as a support system for children in need. An organization like DCYF, one who has dedicated to itself to the protection of the youth, deserves some recognition. When Write Bloody asked for an organization to associate my poem with for this anthology, I knew that DCYF would be getting all the attention I could give it.

DEUS EX MACHINA

It was this close he says, squeezing a small ball
of air between thumb & index. The officer
fishes bullet from gypsum burrow,
a mole on the ivory wall's pristine face.

His flashlight sweeps across kitchen
a swamp of broken china, hovers
above my father's would be grave.

Down the hall, threads of light crochet
a dark room. My bloody hand opens
a bible. I imagine lead steeds
galloping through gun smoke
into a corral of meat & bone. Before,

we planted swollen fingers
around dinner, our bodies upright
sacks of coal praising the heat of his belt,
I clasped my hands, eyes shut. a prayer–
It was this close

- Mckendy Fils-Aimé

MEG DAY

Meg Day, selected for *Best New Poets of 2013*, is a 2013 recipient of an NEA Fellowship in Poetry and the author of *Last Psalm at Sea Level* (winner of Barrow Street Press' first book prize in poetry), *When All You Have Is a Hammer* (winner of the 2012 Gertrude Press Chapbook Contest) and *We Can't Read This* (winner of the 2013 Gazing Grain Chapbook Contest). A 2012 AWP Intro Journals Award Winner, she has also received awards and fellowships from the Lambda Literary Foundation, Hedgebrook, Squaw Valley Writers, and the International Queer Arts Festival. Meg is currently a Steffensen-Cannon Fellow, Point Foundation Scholar, & PhD candidate in Poetry & Disability Poetics at the University of Utah. www.megday.com

The Network/La Red
http://www.tnlr.org

The Network/La Red: Survivor-led Organizing to End Partner Abuse is a phenomenal organization based out of Boston, Massachusetts that focuses on the lesbian, gay, bisexual, transgender, BDSM, polyamorous, and queer communities. As their mission statement says, they are rooted in anti-oppression principles and aim to create a world where all folks are free from oppression. What's exceptional about this org is that all of their services are free, confidential, bilingual, and accessible—they make a point to prioritize the needs of the community & provide ASL interpreting. Founded in 1989, The Network/La Red started the #iwantaworld campaign, which you should definitely check out, and encourages you to become involved via donation, volunteer opportunities, & internships. Organizations like this one are so unique in that they meet communities and individuals where they're at instead of trying to provide cookie-cutter information and assistance. You can check them out, educate yourself, or find a hotline at www.tnlr.org

GHAZAL FOR FINALLY LEAVING WHAT HAS ALREADY LEFT

I imagine there were angels once, or at least the sound of them,
trumpeting some broken hallelujah against the ceiling above that bed.

There must have been electricity – a current – to power
the elaborate maneuvering that kept me fastened to that bed.

I don't remember much: the arrivals & departures blurred as healing
scars
& the kitchen always quiet. There was little concern for bedlam or
bedtime

& the mornings it snowed kept me close to the windows, screens
thawing –
like my want – wired & damp. At night, a phantom weight beside me
in the bed.

I imagine spring could have begun kindly & coaxed the steady stride
of summer into its measured snare – an entire season of sickness,
bed-

bound alone with The Book of Hours – then swung hard into
September,
pocket watches leaned open in palms like old men in gold rockers;
beds

like deep yawns, yawns like gaping coffins. Lord, what was I
but made in your image: invisible. I come to you a cavern of bedrock,

rendered acquiescent. I arrive secondhand. You, Lord, are the woman
I longed to be
or be with, the walking ache of so many confessions, the merciful

depository embedded
in surrender. Come: weep in my arms. If you are the beginning &
end, then let us be
what we are best: the slow departure, the unlikely subsistence,
bedmates without a bed.

- Meg Day

ROBBIE Q. TELFER

Robbie Q. Telfer is the co-founder and curator for The Encyclopedia Show, a live literary variety show being staged independently in over 10 cities around the world. He's been in two documentaries (from HBO and Siskel and Jacobs) for his work at Young Chicago Authors where he organized the world's largest teen poetry festival called Louder Than A Bomb. He's written on two video games, was the poetry correspondent for *TimeOut Chicago*, and his first published book of poetry, *Spiking the Sucker Punch*, was released in 2009 from Write Bloody Publishing. He's currently a Poet-in-Residence in the Poetry Center of Chicago's Hands on Stanzas program.

Cure Violence
http://cureviolence.org/

Featured in the documentary **The Interrupters**, Cure Violence works to diffuse potentially violent situations in communities across the country. By giving tools to communitiesand training individuals, they are able to diminish the impact of stressors that lead to violence.

KIDS KILLING KIDS

Written in part from this video produced by my colleagues at
Free Spirit Media: http://www.youtube.com/watch?v=jxpAV0-lxLo

I turn 30 years old this year
that is just a symptom but not
the disease.
They say it is not one thing.
Aging for me has always meant
expanding. When I was 12
and puberty detonated
inside me, my world was only
family, people behind cash
registers, and the 31 kids
in my 7th grade class.
If I had thought to be reckless
I would have.
I am not reckless.
I am still a child.
I am expanding.
My world is – by comparison to
my 1993 me – giant, soul-
haltingly huge, perhaps
it is as big as the entire Earth,
but probably is just the size
of the Northside of Chicago,
yes, my world is not the size
of the Earth.

They say it is not one thing
this sad, this tragic, this
devastation of another world
another planet in this city.

In the 7th grade, I believed in
magic, or what is more accurately
called "the force." I believed in
the power of feeling so hard
at something it would perceive
my feelings, be hypnotized by them,
and would react to my wishes
in kind:
- I felt at the Bulls, and they won.
- I felt at pencils on my desk, and they did not fly into my hand.
- I felt at girls. I felt at so many girls.
There was no time to say or
do anything – all my time was
spent working... on the force.

They say it is not one thing
36 Chicago Public School kids dead in 2009
50% graduation rate for CPS students
dropouts more likely to be murdered
it is not one thing
40% of handgun sales in Illinois
made without a background check
because of a legal loophole.
Developmental distress caused by
poor nutrition, food deserts, negative
parenting, schools like prisons, friends
getting slaughtered, why would
parents be negative?

I went to a school last month
every eighth window a garbage
bag. Cops in the classroom.
A teacher told a girl she had
a fat ass and he looked at me
and laughed. A kid told me

he was on the street and
a cop picked him up and
dropped him off in rival gang
territory.
No one listened to my lecture
on the first amendment.

I felt awful and exhausted
I drove back to my side
I feel like shit
and unless you're a racist
you feel like shit too.

I turn 30 this year
and at least once a day
I feel bad.
I hear something and I feel
bad. I point my bad feelings
South
and then come back to my side
and work has been done
and I haven't had to do anything
and I haven't had to say anything
I just point my feelings
I just use the force
and I've done work.
White guilt is hard work.

When the work is done
I have a sense of accomplishment
sure the disease isn't cured
but I went to a variety show
and felt bad for a whole hour,
what's on MythBusters?

I mean to be preachy so forgive me
but
perhaps maybe you could volunteer for
a community organization?
perhaps maybe you could donate to
groups for handgun prevention?
perhaps maybe you could redefine
separate but equal for 2010?
perhaps maybe we should consider
them kids before they're murdered?
they say it is not one thing but
perhaps maybe it is one thing
perhaps maybe it is power
perhaps maybe it has always been power
perhaps maybe you could loosen your grip
on power
perhaps definitely everyone reading this
is one of the 10% richest people in the world
perhaps maybe feeling bad isn't work.
At all.

I turn 30 years old this year
I am still a child
my world expands hourly
I'm going to die definitely

If I were a fortune cookie right now
and you cracked me open
the little paper would say:
Accept what you can't control
Do something about what you can
12, 30, 100 — you're lucky
please share some of your fortune.

- *Robbie Q. Telfer*

ASAD ALVI

Asad Alvi is a spoken word artist and writer from Karachi, Pakistan. He has helped conduct and facilitate fiction writing workshops at Open Letters, a growing society of creatively-driven writers. His work has been published in an anthology of short stories by the Oxford University Press (OUP), launched at the 5th Karachi Literature Festival in 2014. His work can be found on www.rantdoms.wordpress.com

Spoken Stage
https://www.facebook.com/spokenstage

The women of Pakistan bear the brunt of poor governance, military strife, and the corruption of the social, political and economic systems which surround them. Women make up 49% of the population of Pakistan, yet they are continuously marginalized and discriminated against by the middle class and feudal societies, and through political and social structures which are inherently misogynistic and patriarchal. 'The Crossroads' is a character study of one such woman and studies the subtle ways in which she is a victim of her own silence. The issue is important to me because my own mother has been a victim of patriarchy, and it has taken her immense strength to break free. And so, this poem, in its own self, is a defiance of sorts. It is for her. I want to say that.

Spoken Stage is an organization that develops and promotes performance poetry/storytelling performance art and encourages freedom of expression in Pakistan. It provides emerging writers with opportunities, events and activities, and helps them explore the endless potential of poetry as a tool for social change. In the past, it has organized spoken word evenings where writers have brought important social issues such as bullying and early marriages to light.

THE CROSSROADS.

They take the highway going north-west;
the one which meets the ancient barrage.
At Kotri, they shall take the infamous pull
built above the waterway, and park there.

Then from there, catching the local boat,
plying them to Sukkur nearly by midnight;
When the north stars scuffles at the skies;
The hosts will be lighting all the lamps.

Now he, dressed in a crisp, blue sweater
Which his mother knitted last September.
Fingers flaked jet black with raw tobacco
from hand-made, sharp-rolled cigarettes.

She, yet new to his subtle, blunt intricacy
sees them with a quieted, long glance,
guiding herself through the still moment;
She wishes she was more sure of herself.

Perhaps more attention to his details will
teach, she reassuringly tells herself, how
wives do go about in such troubled times,
when one can't yet see the crossing-line.

At a gas-station the car halts, afterwards.
He climbs out, a certain shade of sunlight
hitting him, like two ends come complete.
The woman sits with sore legs in the back,
Staring outside; her left eye swollen blue.

And then, the passerby upon the crossing.
He's wearing one of those shirts you'd see

on the roadside vendor stalls; tanned skin.
His smile reminds the woman of someone.

The man emptying crumped bills from his
pocket, returns to the car, bolting the door
tightly, driving away. And the passerby on
the crossing, fades away into the evening.

It has begun to rain now; raindrops falling
on the wind-shield are shining like pearls.
She wipes away her tears with her shawl –
And no more Karachi following her.

– Asad Alvi

MEGAN FALLEY

Megan Falley is the author of two full-length collections of poetry, After the Witch Hunt (2012) and Redhead and the Slaughter King (2014) both published by Write Bloody. She won the Tired Hearts Open Chapbook Contest with a manuscript of poems about Lana Del Rey. In addition to writing books, Megan tours nationally and teaches a course online called "Poems That Don't Suck."

Hollaback
http://www.ihollaback.org

Hollaback! is an organization devoted to end street harassment. Living in New York City, street harassment is something I experience every day, and the damages of it often permeate into my work. I'd love to help end street harassment so that I can write about something new and feel safe walking in whatever I feel like wearing.

BACKHANDED APOLOGY

I am sorry I am woman. Sorry for the cicadas of my chest, how they hibernated for thirteen years, then ruined your summer. Sorry for each freckle on my shoulder—speckles of dirt in your pancake batter. Sorry the high school banned tank tops so you could concentrate on your math. Sorry I bled on your couch. Sorry I didn't tell you, flipped the cushion upside-down. Sorry I grow hair, like you. Sorry that even in television commercials for women's razors it's always a bare, bronzed leg being shaved. Sorry I'm not already all the way removed. Sorry for walking down the street wearing that skirt. Sorry for the minutes it took out of your workday to gawk like that. To say those things. Sorry I didn't say, *Thank you*. I thought you were going to kill me. Sorry I keep my mail, front door, and apartment key between each of my fingers when I walk. Sorry I say sorry so much. Sorry you got fired for grabbing my ass like it was the candy on my desk. Of course it belonged to you. Sorry for all the ridiculous laws—of gravity too—I'm sure my breasts are very happy to see you. Sorry you liked breast milk so much. Sorry I fed you in public and let everyone know you loved a woman then. Sorry I was your first home and didn't leave my body open for you to crawl back in. Sorry that the egg that made me came from inside my mother when she was inside her mother. Sorry for all this forever. Sorry you're on the outside of the joke. Sorry I bled on your couch and I didn't turn over the cushion this time.

- Megan Falley

AS THE SEA WALKS TOWARDS US

NATALIE E. ILLUM

Natalie E. Illum is a performance poet, disability activist and storyteller living in Washington, DC. She is a founding board member of the mothertongue poetry series, a women's open mic that lasted 15 years. Her work has appeared the anthologies *Word Warriors: 35 Women of the Spokenword Revolution; Full Moon on K Street; Feminist Studies* and on NPR's *Snap Judgment*. She has competed on the National Poetry Slam circuit since 2008, and is the 2013 Beltway Grand Slam Champion. She is also a contributing writer for the *Huffington Post* and the *Stop The Beauty Madness* Campaign. You can follow her at www. natalieillum.net and @poetryrox on Twitter and Instagram.

The Body Is Not An Apology
http://www.thebodyisnotanapology.com/

The poem "Don't Look At Me" was written in 2008. I wanted to write about the underbelly of my disability, beyond the crutches, wheelchair, or metaphor. It was the first poem where I really exposed myself and then tried to end with some hope, because the poem needed it and so did I. Once upon a time, Sonya Renee Taylor and I were on a slam team together and I fell in our hotel room. I couldn't stop saying sorry for making us late. She asked me why I kept apologizing for my body. I didn't have an answer. The Body Is Not An Apology is a radical self-love movement founded by Sonya Renee Taylor in 2011. Sonya's words and work helped me truly stop apologizing for the body I live in, whatever the condition, the damage. There is always beauty. Now, I see it.

From their website: "The Body Is Not An Apology is a GLOBAL movement focused on radical self-love and body empowerment. We believe that each time you unapologetically own your beauty, love your scars, heal your shame; you in turn give us permission to do the same!"

DON'T LOOK AT ME

Sometimes what I want most is
to be a wallflower; invisible.
The first scar I remember was

from the parking lot of the Ground Round.
I was pushing my walker too fast
for kindergarten, split
my chin on the crossbar
but missed that slice
of party pizza.

Fast forward 5 years
to the dent on my forehead
or my tooth chipped
on the radiator in the same week.

On my 13th birthday it's my mother's fist
sending my head into the kitchen table
left me shaken and bloody in the bathtub
refusing to stitch that moment up.
I know

you don't what to hear this but
know this: disability isn't pretty.
It's permanent captivity.
It's the body held hostage
by your own nervous system.

It's never be able to run
from the damage
in your own brain.
Even when
I grew some serious cleavage,
boosted my confidence
with a Wonder Bra.

Even when I perfected
blow jobs because
I'd be kneeling
and he'd be too distracted
to notice

how my feet twist outward
and my shoulders curve
like guardrails.

I know the high beams of your staring
like I know the scars that crest up my thighs
like a warning:

I am an accident. You can't help but
rubberneck at the scrap metal mess.
I was 2 years old when they severed
my hamstrings. I was 20 when

the doctors told me it was a bad call.
I was 25 when I stopped believing
I was some kind of alternative

Wonder Woman who could still fly.

Don't call me courageous. I don't
want your pity
like a bouquet of roses.
And I don't want
another 1 night stand
to save me from
the full length mirror
in the morning.
Sometimes what I want most

is to go back

37 years to the ICU
to find that girl
who fit in the palm
of her mother's hand
with skin like blue paper.

Sometimes what I want most
is to ask her why
she stayed; cradled
in I.V. lines and fighting

when it would have been
so easy to
just let go.

Will she tell me why
we all struggle
in the limbo
of our own bodies?

Will she give me
enough strength
to hold on to
my own sanity?

She opens her eyes, says
look at me.

What I want most
is for you to understand
we are never too broken
for this world.

– Natalie E. Illum

JESSE PARENT

Jesse Parent placed 2nd at both the 2010 and 2011 Individual World Poetry Slams, was a finalist at the 2012 Ontario International Poetry Slam, and was part of the 8th place Salt City Slam teams at the 2011 and 2012 National Poetry Slams. He has been on the 2007-2014 Salt City Slam teams, has served as SlamMaster and coach for Salt City Slam, and has served on the executive council for Poetry Slam, Inc. He is the author of *The Noise That Is Not You*, a full length book of poetry published by Sargent Press. http://www.jesseparent.com

I wrestled in high school and college, and weight and body control were constantly on my mind. I've intentionally stopped subscribing to mens fitness magazines and other publications that promote an ideal male body image, as well as watch documentaries like *I Want to Look Like That Guy* and *Bigger Stronger Faster* to get a more realistic sense of what it takes to craft that ideal image, but it is still difficult to see myself as less than what I should be.

You can find out more about body dysmorphic disorder in men at: http://www.ncbi.nlm.nih.gov/pmc/articles/PMC1121529/

DYSMORPHIA

I turn my mirrors into jewelers' loupes
able to magnify the smallest flaw.
I wield a chisel that widens confidence cracks,
a recession in my self worth.

My lens is tinted
putting blind spots on points of pride,
forgetting the facets that catch the light,
until all that comes through
are the defects of my tiny calves.
Miniscule and hidden by self-effacing comments
and a fear of wearing shorts.
My belly that will never
crosshatch out abdominal definition,
constantly keeping me from shirtlessness.
My tattoos safe from the sun.
Body hair ironically twisted into baldness.
Feast and famine.
Junk jewelry.

I wallow laying prone in isolation,
no longer bothered by the presence of my ego.
Growing fat on my insecurities
dripping grease on the corner of my mouth.
I have made myself into a funhouse.
Warping.

If only mirrors were made from my children's eyes.
Maybe then I would see the image God cast of himself.
Maybe then I could see something worthwhile
not mere costume jewelry, but a diamond,
shining and beautiful to untrained eyes.
My children make me into gems,

embedded into crowns and scepters.
Proclaim me priceless,
instead of this blend of optics and imagination
that I find so lacking.
A mustard tree planted
from a seed of doubt,
resistant to the herbicide of praise and assurances.

This is not bait for compliments.
I am incapable of landing them.
Although I believe in the power of words
I don't believe any of you.
You are seeing someone different than I am.
I have spent my life
inspecting this form with jeweler's loupes,
reinforced by every Men's Fitness magazine
that advertises week long workout routines
guaranteed to make me look like
the quietly anabolic cover models
as if the chiseled features of their bodies
occurred in nature.
Their images Photoshopped onto
the Polaroid pictures in my brain
that dictate the jewel I should look like.
instead of this a dull ore,
merely mined.

All the work of my loved ones,
my friends,
who polish me with soft cloths of kind words
like a child's precious bauble,
is easily undone.

One harsh word penetrates layers of kind ones
like a bullet through felt.

Self-inflicted.
This oaf, this thing.
Unrefined.
Fragile being.

I am no diamond,
I break like glass.

– Jesse Parent

JACLYN WEBER

Jaclyn Weber is a California native with a BS in English, Creative Writing from Bradley University. She has work published in *The Feminist Wire, NonBinary Review* and *Zaum Literary Magazine*. Jaclyn has performed her work across the Midwest at universities such as Cornell College, The University of Illinois at Springfield, Upper Iowa's Fine Arts Series and manymore. http://jaclynweber.com/

The Beautiful Cervix Project
http://www.beautifulcervix.com

The grassroots movement, The Beautiful Cervix Project, celebrates the beauty of women's bodies and promotes healing through experiencing one's own body. Armed with a mirror and plastic speculum, The Beautiful Cervix Project is the inspiration between the lines of my poem, reminding myself everyday that I am the most important person in my life.

ME, MYSELF AND VIBE

May 2013 was the first official masturbate-a-thon.
"I tell people it's like a walk-a-thon, except at the end your feet don't
hurt...
unless you masturbate in a very unusual fashion."

Go figure, National Masturbation Month is during my birthday
month.
I gained 10 pounds,
ended up single, and adopted a cat named Sugar Puss.

Tonight, I'm going to light a few candles,
pour myself some cabernet, put on Barry White,
slide over the bed and whisper to my wine bottle,
"Shh...baby, you're going to help make this night interesting...
wait one moment while I go get some new batteries."

I'm 24, still single and just want to mingle with my fingers.
Sorry if that makes you uncomfortable
and excuse me for not shaking hands.

Porn is just not cutting it.
You know, the one where the girls are in the boys' locker room,
naked,
making out, spanking each other?
Oh, you haven't seen that one? No girl, it's okay.
Ask your boyfriend...he has.
See, look at his eyes shifty as shit.
I need to save my strength for my vibrator grip.

Doing myself has its plusses:
the mess is contained; I don't care if I haven't shaved for three days
and I know what dirty talk I like, "You want some chicken?"
The biggest plus?

It was big enough and I didn't have to suck.
The pamphlet claims we women,
"need to feel more comfortable masturbating."
A recent study counts on one hand
all the girls who've fingered themselves into believing
their bodies are not cervix beautiful.
Taught not to reflect the mirror down
our other half.

And I'll count to five and vibrate all the reasons why
I don't give a shit what you think about my body
or what God I shout to.
When I climax, I'm on my own and
I moan at what I've created
with my own two hands,

without help from *Cosmopolitan's* 25 streaming, sexy
luscious masturbation tips to touch yourself,
to love myself on May 27, 2013.
I'll take off all my clothes and stay home
with me, myself and a bottle of fine lady lube.
I'll ask myself how I want it and I'll remember.

– Jaclyn Weber

J.A. CARTER-WINWARD

*** The author would like to attribute the beginning quotation to Dr. Carol Queen.

J.A. Carter-Winward is the author of *Grind: a Novel, No Secrets (poetry), No Apologies (poetry), Shorts: a Collection, The Rub: a Novel, Falling Back to Earth,* and *TDTM.* She lives and writes in the mountains of Northern Utah. www.jacarterwinward.com

National Organization of Women Foundation: Love Your Body
http://now.org/now-foundation/love-your-body/

From the time we are young, women in America are taught to hate our bodies. We have 'too much of this, too little of that.' When we aren't seeing the barrage of media images, we are hearing the criticism from people who have bought into the impossible ideal of female perfection. The consumer market is inundated with products that rely on our self-loathing to make billions each year. The particular group to which I belong is impacted two-fold: not only are we held to a standard of beauty, but of youth as well. And youth, no matter how hard we try, cannot be purchased. I wrote my poem, *Grace,* to reveal my personal epiphany with this issue of beauty and youth. I chose the National Organization of Women's *Love Your Body* movement because it is the only organization existing that advocates for all women in all stages of life and in every permutation of beauty, no matter how she measures up to the warped ideal our society has embraced. We must speak up. We must start with ourselves and embrace female beauty as something that is found on the inside and in the diversity that is All Women. It's time we are valued for who we really are, what we really look like, and reject what our society has attempted to make us.

GRACE

at the medical spa, i stood in line to buy
low-carb, low-calorie, high-protein quiche.
surrounded by boxes and tinctures of hope--
lose weight, remain ageless, revisit youth--
a serum to erase the lines
earned in the sun or by laughter
or genes—by life.

a woman stood next to me
filling out a form inviting the needles in
botulism in a box to make the wrinkles disappear.
wearing a maid's uniform, hair back in a ponytail
she'd been cleaning houses all day to support her habit of youth.
i brought my hand up to my face and felt the softness there,
the heavy lines where my smile has left traces,
trails i can follow with my thoughts leading
to the fondest memories
and belly laughs and joy.
no, i would not erase the physical evidence
no more than i
could destroy an ancient rock with striated lines revealing prehistoric
rivers and early sun-baked clay.

another woman came in and i looked at her face.
an anomaly,
like a graffitied wall plopped in the center
of a pristine mountain meadow.
her skin too pink, pulled tight, preternaturally shiny
as if an artist's brush had glazed
the surface of her face to a sheen.
places that should have sunk in
puffed out like phyllo dough,
her lips were in a pout, like a petulant child's.

as if she were a toppled car on a highway shoulder,
i searched for the cracks in the windshield to see if something
resembling
human
rested inside.

i am no paragon of aging gracefully.
i cover my gray roots in dye,
i battle my mid-section with daily crunches
and low-carb quiche.
i feel my half-century mark looming ahead of me
like a tombstone waiting for the last vestiges
of my youth to
tumble into its dark hole.

i sat in the bath
cradling my belly, looking down at my breasts—
i had seen the alternatives to aging with grace.
i suddenly couldn't wait for those shy white strands of hair
to run rampant and take over.
the pressure to be a certain way--
the constant hum of fear gave
sway
to acceptance of that life-changing,
yet plodding movement into being
mature,
past my prime—
older.

comfortable shoes!
billowy blouses!
mismatched scarves that clash with my pants!
being seen through a lens of who i am
not what i look like or my fuckability.
i pulled my hands up and over my supple skin and felt the weight
of all of those expectations

lift in increments as if borne up by helium.

and yet, i must give my youth the chance to peter out on its own.
my gray hair isn't ready to take over just yet.
my lines and wrinkles are not so set in stone.
but i no longer fear this final emergence
into womanhood that has haunted me for so long.
i watch the door for this part of myself,
waiting with eager, open arms,
and when she comes we will be friends--
we will clasp hands and speak of days past
when we relied on our beauty
too much,
when we didn't rely on
our *selves* enough,
and we will cackle at the freedom given to us
by the passage of time.

– J.A. Carter-Winward

NIC ALEA

Nic Alea is a Bay Area-based writer and co-founder of the New Sh!t Show, an open mic celebrating the production of new work. Nic's poems have been published in *Word Riot, The Legendary, Rattle,* and *Muzzle Magazine.* Nic is a 2012 Lambda Literary Fellow and was recently voted one of SF Weekly's "Best Writers without a Book."

More information at poetrynicalea.wordpress.com.

The Body Is Not An Apology
http://www.thebodyisnotanapology.com

The journey of healing is one that can be lonesome and exhausting without support and affirmations. Sonya Renee Taylor, an incredible poet and organizer, began the Body is Not an Apology from a poem of the same name. This global organization makes room for dialogue and unapologetic ownership of our bodies. TBINAA is a vital organization for all different types of communities. When we say yes to our bodies, our genders, our race, our bad days and good days, we are saying yes to undoing patriarchal standards and instead choosing love.

THUNDER THIGHS

Ballooning out from your denim,

your work boots, your high heels,

those cottage cheese limbs tackling your bones,

you, growing up and outward, girl, boy, I see you.

When the girls turned their jaws

like weather vanes to smirk at my gut,

to tell me my belly is covered in state lines,

looks like maps and horrible highways,

that my tits sag like a bad joke,

that somehow I am warm milk,

my jelly roll undeserving,

clogging itself in a burden of scratch marks,

pulls at the skin, sparks thunder, a fleshy flint,

the kind of ripple that look like sand when it's disturbed.

Here's me in a floral head wreath

trying for days to be a porcelain doll,

to climb the mountain without busting out this flab,

whale bones, elephant tusks, beans crushed under my fists,

I am learning how to say I love you and mean it,

but today I feel fat and not in the fun way.

It is a miracle to be complicated and stagnant,

to book the date of the surgery, to pull at the skin,

to call yourself prom queen and then burn the dress.

My sweet flabby pies grinning with electric lips and tornado want,

my belt buckle bulging like a rose about to burst,

smell suckle, smell like salt flat and human being,

digging up crystals to give light from the folds in my belly,

I am not fat because the middle school boys used to tell me I am,

I just am.

So here's you in a dim lit bedroom with your magic down

and your voice cracking like ice on sweet grass,

so we say together, Thunder Thighs,

you god damn love story,

you perfectly gendered slabs of meat,

you craters of skin that just can't get enough of each other,

I see you.

– Nic Alea

JOANNA HOFFMAN

Joanna Hoffman ranked 4th at the 2012 Women of the World Poetry Slam and she represented Urbana at the 2011 Women of the World Poetry Slam (WOWPS), National Poetry Slam, and Individual World Poetry Slam, placing in the top 10 at all three. Her work has appeared in publications including *PANK*, *decomP*, *Union Station Magazine*, *Drunk in a Midnight Choir*, *The New*, and *The Legendary*, and her full-length book of poetry, *Running for Trap Doors*, was released by Sibling Rivalry Press in 2013. She has been nominated for a Pushcart and a Lambda Literary Award.

American Cancer Society
www.cancer.org

The American Cancer Society is a nationwide, community-based voluntary health organization dedicated to eliminating cancer as a major health problem. Headquartered in Atlanta, Georgia, the ACS has regional and local offices throughout the country that support 11 geographical Divisions and ensure ACS has a presence in every community.

CROWN CINQUAIN FOR CHEMO

The first
time I saw her
without hair, I thought of
how a rot trunk made god call for
wildfire.

Chemo
shivers all the
portraits back into scrawl.
We store her eyelashes in jars
and pray.

Doctors
tell us *Your mom
is a fighter. Against
which war?* I want to ask but keep
silent.

The wig,
a false prophet.
The chemo port, a lost
highway. My god, a bribe to fill
the hours.

The first
tuft of hair came
like smoke after the bang.
No blond curls. Straight grey, a weary
white flag.

– Joanna Hoffman

ERIC SILVER

Eric Silver is the co-founder and four-time team member of Slam! at NYU, the most winningest collegiate slam poetry team. A recipient of the Emerging Jewish Artist Fellowship from the Bronfman Center, he self-published the first run of his chapbook *Post-Awkward Expressionism*. A high school English teacher and cardigan enthusiast, he wants to be somewhere between Robin Williams in *Dead Poets' Society* and College *Dropout* Kanye.

National Eating Disorder Association
https://www.nationaleatingdisorders.org/

Enhancing Male Body Image
https://www.nationaleatingdisorders.org/enhancing-male-body-image

Help Line Information: 800.931.2237

The "Enhancing Male Body Image" page on the National Eating Disorder Association website is the most straightforward affirmation of a male body image I have ever read. And I have searched. Set up as a series of guidelines, it lays out what every man should do to appreciate himself and his physicality. No awkwardness, no shame, no questions – just a list for figuring it out. Maybe it won't hurt so much tomorrow, maybe the pushups can be for me and not the love I think I'll receive, maybe I can hold my gaze in the mirror a little longer. The entire section for male eating disorders and body dysmorphia is extremely comprehensive, and the entire website and organization is working towards empowering and encouraging love for all bodies.

KNICK

I have only one distinct memory of my dad trying to explain
sex to me. My brother and I sit with him in a booth at our go-
to fake Italian restaurant. Halfway through scouring the
breadbasket, he says, "So, do you know how sex works?" And
my brother and I say yes, because we sit with the cool kids
a back of the bus. And he says, "Well, uh, when the penis
gets hard, it's so you can, you know, stick it in the woman."
And we, as 12-year-olds who cannot fathom adult bodies
properly, ew loud enough to rattle the glassware.

The problem with being somebody who craves another and
also hates his body is that I know what will ruin the night.
Every burst of warmth, every gnaw of lip vibrates alongside
an apology. I am sorry I've convinced you into this nest
of flesh, that you've been duped by jokes and so much smiling.
You will discover too late how my tender is uncertain. How
my excitement is a bathtub overflowing. I'm sorry I am the
door prize you have won: an orchestra of clumsy. I may crush
you if my arms give out. I am sorry for how my sweat has
doused the sheets. For the questions: Is this okay? What can I
do? Are you enjoying yourself? I am sorry I need love to
become a mantra. You will stay. You will stay. You will stay.
If you say it enough times, it won't mean anything in your
mouth. I am trying to get you used to that inevitability. I am
sorry I will wake you to check if you've changed your mind
overnight.

When I unbutton, even alone, I believe I am overstaying my
welcome. I wash every stitch of myself in angry awe. I test the
weight of another in my arms, like if I can hold her, the bulk
can be forgiven. According to what I have learned, I am doing
it right. But I do not know how to forgive what I have been
hauling around. In bed, where I should drop everything else,

I call myself burden. I cannot unzip the guilt, the mistake, the confusion in my face. I believe I am accidental cut, a knick into the meat of the thumb when slicing something else.

— *Eric Silver*

PATRICK HOLLOWAY

Patrick Holloway is a young Irish writer currently completing his PhD in creative writing in Brazil. His poetry and fiction has been published by *Poetry Ireland Review* and *Overland Literary Journal*, among others. He is currently completing a bilingual book of poetry.

BeatBullying
http://www.beatbullying.org

BeatBullying is an international bullying prevention organization working and campaigning to make bullying unacceptable, on the ground in the UK and across Europe.

They believe that no one should endure the pain, fear or isolation of being bullied, and that everyone has the right to be safe from bullying, violence and harassment.

BeatBullying stops bullying and keeps young people safe.

A RITUAL

In the cold changing room
I wait behind
While the other boys
Run towards the sea
All zipped up.

You open the door slowly and peek
Around to make sure it's just me
And I nod and then you walk
Towards me with a smile that looks
More like a cry.

We don't say a word as I slowly
Zip the wetsuit up over your
Back, pushing the fat this way and
That until finally with one last pull
The zip fastens.

We walk towards the sea as the sea
Walks towards us.

– Patrick Holloway

JENNIFER JACKSON BERRY

Jennifer Jackson Berry is the author of the chapbooks When I Was a Girl (Sundress Publications, 2014), which is available at http://www.sundresspublications.com/echaps.htm, and Nothing But Candy (Liquid Paper Press, 2003). She is an Assistant Editor for WomenArts Quarterly Journal and lives in Pittsburgh, Pennsylvania.

WEBSITE: jaxnberry.tumblr.com
TWITTER: @jaxnberry

Resolve: The National Infertility Association
http://www.resolve.org

There is great stigma and silence surrounding the issue of infertility, yet one out of every eight U.S. couples of childbearing age is diagnosed with infertility. I write about my and my husband's struggles to break the silence. RESOLVE: The National Infertility Association was established in 1974 and promotes reproductive health and works to ensure equal access for all family building options for men and women experiencing infertility or other reproductive disorders with support groups, educational programs, and advocacy initiatives.

POST-MISCARRIAGE: DAY 55

I can't wear the red
sweater anymore.

I've been getting emails
about cord blood.

I wonder if it's redder,
thicker, darker

than mother's blood,
is it *more?*

I lost weight from eating
healthy & learning

to control my sugars.
Wouldn't you want

when you're pregnant sweet,
sweet blood?

I will always confuse
succor & sucra-.

I read about the dangers
of artificial sweeteners then.

I read more into that red
sweater picture now.

It was Christmas.
No one knew.

I looked good at that party.
I didn't think I had that glow,

so early in the pregnancy.
I had too much

to think about, already
too much weight.

– Jennifer Jackson Berry

GREG HARRIES

Greg Harries is the Artistic Director of RESPECT, a social justice theater group, and a teaching artist with the Nebraska Writers Collective, in Omaha, Nebraska. He started writing poetry in 2012 to prove to his Louder Than a Bomb students that he was more than just a theater kid. Every day of his writing since then has been spent trying to chase their fearlessness.

National Sleep Foundation
http://www.sleepfoundation.org

The National Sleep Foundation is an indispensable resource for people suffering from sleep disorders and struggles. We spend a third of our lives sleeping, but rarely does it get the health focus that we dedicate to diet and exercise. SleepFoundation.org features resources for moderating your own sleep health, and a database of professionals that can provide more intense care as needed.

STRATEGY GUIDE

On my family's Nintendo
I could never play Dr. Mario.
The viral enemies and the player capsules
are all yellow, blue, or red.
Line up any four blocks of the same color and they disappear,
your pills taking grinning viruses
with them in kamikaze simplicity.
I could never solve those puzzles.
I'd gum the onscreen bottle up,
Game Over, every time.
My mom, though, she was a nurse,
and she was a pro.
She could maneuver pills with pinpoint precision,
plan ahead with the preview window,
yellow, blue, and red fell from her thumbtips oh-so easily.

She left us, though, when her own sickness got too thick,
in a pattern too insidious, its grinning faces
digging wriggling cilia into the bottle of her body.
Yellow: no sleep for days over first son in hospital.
Blue: no sleep for more days over next son in police custody.
Red: a ragged new voice whispering at the edges of all of that pain.
It filled her up, it blocked the mouth of her bottle,
the red voice grabbed her hand,
made it grab pill bottles, upending them into the toilet.

The red voice writhed into her throat, then.
I'd spend hours held tight to her in her bedroom,
my father outside sitting against the wall,
listening through the cracks in the locked door
as she murmured into my nine-year-old ear
bedtime stories about his anger, of how he longed to hurt us,
of how the only safe place from his rage was with her,

lies that only the red voice would ever believe.
I know this, I promise, I swear.

After just days of this, the ambulance came
and took her away
to a place where the sickness
couldn't block the mouth of her bottle with its jitterbug strut,
couldn't keep the pills out, from ending its mad dance,
couldn't stop my mother from bravely unclenching the red voice's
grip.
For months, she learned how to drop pills from her thumbtips again.
Yellow, blue, red, purple, white, white and red, green, orange, blue,
blue, blue
into daily pill organizers. Her thumbtips grasped tight around the red
voice's throat.
For those same months, I learned how to pick at my nails, like my
mom always has.
For years, I learned how to never stop picking at my nails, like my
mom never has.
For decades, I learned how to sleep
just enough.

We don't play Dr. Mario in my family anymore.
Now Mom plays Cooties with her grandkids,
they roll their dice, they find their parts,
they make their little plastic bugs complete.
Across the family room, I sit by the warmth of the fireplace
vigilant. Listening for the red voice at the edges of hers.
And fearing the day that I hear it in mine.

– Greg Harries

ANDREA GIBSON

Andrea Gibson was the first winner of the Women's World Poetry Slam and has headlined prestigious performance venues all over the world with readings on war, class, gender, bullying, white privilege, sexuality, love and spirituality. Gibson has released six full length albums and has published two books, *Pole Dancing to Gospel Hymns,* and *The Madness Vase,* through Write Bloody Publishing.

International Lyme and Associated Diseases Society
http://www.ilads.org

Through education, awareness and action, ILADS promotes the understanding of Lyme Disease and its associated diseases and is dedicated to advancing the standard of care by supporting physician understanding and increasing public awareness.

AN INSIDER'S GUIDE ON HOW TO BE SICK

Never say the words, *This is not my life.*
This pain that wakes you screaming
in the muzzle of the night. That woke
your lover, chased her to another room;
to another life.

This fevered fainting.
This tremoring chest.
The lungs like a mangled kite.
This panic like a cave of bats.

This nurse drawing blood who
wears doubled gloves. This insurance
doesn't cover that. This hurried paycheck
of a doctor after doctor after doctor.

This stethoscope that never hears your heart. This savior
prescription with side effects worse than the disease.
This hospital bed with fluorescent dark. This please
let me have one month where I read
more poems than warning labels. This

not knowing what the tests will say. *This pray pray
pray.* This airplane's medical emergency landing. This
shame when you can't walk. *Shame when you can't
fuck.* Shame when you're home alone sobbing
on another Friday night.

Say, *This is my life.*
This is my precious life.
This is how badly I want to live. Say,

sometimes you have to keep pulling yourself up
by the whip. Take punch after punch
and still uncurl the fist of your grief
like a warm blanket on the cool earth
of your faith. Say, *every waiting room*

is the kiln where you will finally take shape
to fit into the keyhole of your own gritty heart.
To open mercy. To open your siren throat. Say,
every fever is a love note to remind you
there are better things to be than cool.

Fuck cool, fuck every pair of skinny jeans
from the month your muscles started atrophying
to a size two. *Say fuck you* to everyone who asks you
if you eat enough. Say *how do you not know*
that is so fucking rude. *Remember*

you never have an obligation to quiet
the hurricane in your chest, especially
on a day when another healthy person
claims *you would feel so much better if*
you would just focus your breath

into a Buddha beam of light. Like that light
might miraculously dissolve the knife
that's been churning in your kidneys
for the last 6 fucking months. Say,

sunshine please, go back to your job
at the aroma therapy aisle at Whole Foods,
and *leave me alone.* I know how to talk to god,
and right now god does not expect me
to use my inside voice. God knows how
god damn hard I am working to become

a smooth stone. So I can skip

on my back across this red red sea.
So I can trust deep in my screaming
bones everything is a lesson. Lesson
number one through infinity:
You will never have

a greater opportunity to learn to love
your enemy than when your enemy
is your own red blood. *Truce*
is a word made of velvet.
Wear it everywhere you go.

- Andrea Gibson

JACKIE HYMES

Jackie is a poet residing in Los Angeles. She is currently putting the finishing touches on her Master's thesis as California State University, Northridge, where she also teaches first-year composition. Her poem "Plumage" was one of the Honorable Mentions for the Academy of American Poets Prize in 2012 at CSUN and she has also had work published in *Chaparral*. Find more here: http://jackiewritespoems.weebly.com

Hearing Loss Association of America
http://hearingloss.org

Congenital Hearing Loss runs in my family, but I didn't know I had it until I was in kindergarten. At first, I passed every hearing test with flying colors. Yet they wanted to re-test me in an actual audiologist's office. The first test, I faced the audiologist and passed once again; however, when they turned my back to the wall, I failed. As it turns out, my unknown ability to read lips is what enabled me to pass the previous tests. I left the audiologist's office with a letter stating that I needed to wear hearing aids. As a young kindergartner, I cried, thinking, "something is wrong with me." Yet, today I realize the power of reading lips and the beauty in mishearing words. A lot of my images in my poems are born from what I mishear.

The organization I am linking to is the Hearing Loss Association of America. The website provides numerous resources I wish I had taken advantage of when I was younger and lacked self-esteem or confidence because I wore hearing aids. One of the things I particularly enjoy about this website/organization is the advocacy section, which details the rights people with hearing loss are entitled to in different environments. This website also offers a place to connect with other people who have similar hearing loss.

AS EARS LOSE

1.
Speak to me in puzzle.
Let me guess
if *nake* becomes *snake*
by waiting for tongue
to unfurl red carpet.
Let me build
chair out of *air*;
c turns soft as it rests
on h's skeletal body.

2.
Turn to face me.
Allow me to see the sound
of your lips, the pucker
of *w,* the downturned
frown t creates
when it gets past
the picket fence
of your teeth.
Let me see *l*
transform your mouth
into a pop up book
with your tongue
as the tab.

3.
Watch me mistake
the sound of you
silencing
me for a kiss.

— Jackie Hymes

SUSAN VESPOLI

Susan Vespoli lives mainly in Phoenix, but sometimes in Prescott, with her partner and dogs. She has been published in a variety of spots including the *New Verse News, OVS Magazine, Verse Wisconsin* and the soon-to-be-published *Keeping It Weird Portland Anthology*. She is a teacher, poet, and born-again-bicyclist.

Drug Free World
http://www.drugfreeworld.org/drugfacts/prescription-drugs.html

Prescription drug abuse sucks. I have seen those damn little pills eat away at the very essence of some extremely dear individuals. I like this organization because they offer educational information in a non-preachy format.

RISE AND FALL

The Roman Empire. The price of gas.
A glass elevator in a high-rise.
The white Mohawk of waves
continually parting the blue. Surfers
in their slick black suits viewed
from a pier. A fake fur raccoon
tossed into the air by my dog.
A diving board of pigeons facing south
on a street lamp. Alternating legs
of the cloud-haired jogger as he floats
past my window every morning. Cosmos
buds flying from the top of their stems
like helium balloons, like pursed lips,
like fists, opening to drop petals
on the dirt. My hopes for a brilliant addict,
his weight plummeting on a scale, his voice
saying he's just tired. The pill to his lips.
The gravedigger's shovel. A siren wailing
through the morning like a messenger.

- Susan Vespoli

KEN ARKIND

Ken Arkind was born in Routt County, CO, and is the author of *Denver* (Fast Geek Press) and *Coyotes* (Penmanship Books). An American National Poetry Slam Champion, TEDx speaker and Nuyorican Poets Cafe Grand Slam Champion, he has performed his work in 49 States, 6 countries and at over 200 colleges and universities. He is the founding Program Director of Denver Minor Disturbance and the current poetry editor for Suspect Press.https://twitter.com/kenarkind

American Association of University Women
http://www.aauw.org

My mother raised me by herself while trying to negotiate a world that didn't want her to do anything by herself. She, too, along with her two sisters, was raised by a single mother named Eleanor who worked as a mechanic and secretary. Mom was a controller for Red Lion hotels. They often required her to pull 90-100 hour work weeks for a salary that was far less than many of the men in her position. I spent the majority of my early childhood sleeping in the unoccupied rooms of her hotel because she was too busy to come home from her job. My mother was a valedictorian who had received a full scholarship to Cornell University and even as child I knew she was better qualified than most of the men she worked under. When I was 14, she tired of the sexism within the company and literally walked into the GM's office, told him to go fuck himself and promptly left. When she came home, she was laughing so hard I thought she had finally won the lottery. She didn't. In fact, the hardest years of her struggle with this were ahead of her. She survived those, too. I support equal rights and fair wages for all workers.

DIG
for Tonia

Tonia and I are talking about her nipples.

She says that she is thinking of getting them pierced
as a remission present to herself.

Says that she is finished with the knife.

That her last set of treatments will be early next year
and says that her success rate is now 90 to 95 percent.

I ask her if she is considering barbells or rings?

I don't know, which do you think are better?

I tell her that I guess it depends on the size of the nipples.

Well what do you imagine my nipples look like?

I lie,and say that I wouldn't have the slightest idea.

She tells me that they are small but proud.

When even the slightest breeze comes along they stand up,
like soldiers,
and that her new lumpectomy scars remind her of tinsel
lining a pair of sexy Christmas trees.

This statement makes her smile,and I watch the corners of her
mouth stretch out
like a flag greeting the wind.

Earlier in the dayI told her about my mother.

The day she walked out of her jobchin held high as a middle fingerto
the men who refused to pay her what she deserved.

How a year later
she found herself between treatmentssleeping all weekend longbut
somehow still managing to temp 50 hour weeks
while studying for her CPA at night.

She told no one.

Even so, the rumors started to circulate
throughout the cubicles.Whispers hanging in the air
precariously as her wigs.

She decided to settle the rumorsby attending the Halloween
    office party
dressed as Jonathan,the man who shared her cubicle,
and she wore a brown men's suit
with a grey mustacheand a crown of cotton ballsglued to the side of
her bald head.

She laughed all the way to recovery,
even if the others didn't get the joke.

I think of how it has taken her fifty-seven years to find a man
worth building a home with.

The decades of fools who were not strong enough
to understand what all the laughter was about.

This was my model for beauty.

I have never understood the frailness

that so many men search for.

The worship of the thinunblemished arm,the spaghetti strap in place
of the rucksack,
delicate fingersclean nails that have never done digging.

Give me a woman who has lived through
enough disasters to know how to build a shelter.

A woman who bejewels her scars
turns them into precious things
spotlighted in a display caselike a promise
or a warning.

– Ken Arkind

DENISE JOLLY

Denise Jolly is a writer, performer and artist and educator. She is the founder of the Be Beautiful Project, former Executive Director of Seattle Youth Speaks, and Vice President of Stronghold Productions. Denise's work explores the intersections of body, class, sexuality, and gender. Her work has been published on the *Huffington Post, XOJane, HERA Humanities Journal, Cosmopolitan.com* and Write Bloody Publishing's *Courage* anthology. Denise has taught and performed at colleges, universities, community centers, and schools all over the United States and around the world. Denise enjoys working with student populations in elementary through college and beyond. She likes doing great things with amazing people and being moved by art, community and how the two work together to dismantle internalized oppressions.

Harm Reduction Coalition
http://harmreduction.org

Harm Reduction Coalition is a national advocacy and capacity-building organization that promotes the health and dignity of individuals and communities impacted by drug use. Our efforts advance harm reduction policies, practices and programs that address the adverse effects of drug use including overdose, HIV, hepatitis C, addiction, and incarceration. Recognizing that social inequality and injustice magnify drug-related harm and limit the voice of our most vulnerable communities, we work to uphold every individual's right to health and well-being and their competence to participate in the public policy dialogue.

THE RITUAL
for Jill and Norty

The ritual began

with courting a crew of my closest friends.

I knew they were my closest friends

because
they were the people I trusted
with my heart but never my money.

Our catcalls

were a hangdog shoulder
on the North side of school,
service industry smoke
breaks under dim lit awning in a rainstorm,
yellow smoke tail wagging between our fingers.

In the species of us

there was a hunger for
a hug
like head nod of understanding

in the bent crowbar of our half-cocked
necks. Some called this confidence,

others swagger. Most days

it was survival.

When we embraced
we knew
our brothers held us

the way our fathers' heavy hands
taught them to. We could smell it
in the slap skin meat on our necks.

Pretty privileged girls on a junk ride
away from home might call this pheromones,
we understood it as love.

The crew would rally everywhere together
connected at the hip, the hemline,

the jugular taste of uncut.
With this crew every car ride was a mission.

Every mission had a soundtrack.

In the romance of using

we were the stars of a movie,

a tap dancing cliché in a rainstorm
with no chance of lightning.

We were foolishly fearless and brilliant at it.

During the internal negotiation we never called addiction,

shame was a closet of hats
constantly redefining our habits' rationalization.
Cataloging and re-cataloging our history
as if living it wasn't enough the first time.

All of this is to say I have seen some things

that all too often make fireside stories uncomfortable
for those who were raised with much better holding.
Now that I am grown
my days are spent with young folks

trying to pry their way out of shrapnel they call home.
My nights are caught somewhere between

the ideas of what I can be and

the disdain for where I came from.

My best me
exists when pooling
in the massacre that lives
between those two points.

If you have ever bled sunrise
and called it relief. I have compiled a list
of 10 truths I want you to know.
I promise I am still trying to learn myself.

1. You're better than a story about what not to do.

2. You are living in response to your upbringing

which means your children will live in response to how you raise
them.
What do you most want to teach them?

3. Somewhere tonight there is a woman praying for you,
wishing she were your mother.

She knows you might hear her differently
if she were. Do not shun her prayer.
Let it crowbar your liquid shoulders.
We all have rusted parts.

4. Be more than a patina lawn decoration for the wealthy.

5. Some of us have to choose new places to come from.
Do not worry,
you will not forget
what came before that,
it lives
in the fearful cower you'll fight daily.

6. In the moments you forget someone loves you

pretend somewhere across the vast blue
of your compulsion there are continents
of optimist hearts.

7. We humans do get what we ask for.

8. Please stop asking to be re-wounded.

You have branded scars
that will not disappear
with the skin slack of old age.

9. Most days our bodies are temple wars.

Honoring them holy is as much a practice as breathing.

10. Get in the habit of affirming you are holy with each breath.
Brave words like

Loved and Beautiful.

Say

I am holy.

My walls are that of a temple.

I am Sacred.

Sacred does not mean pristine.

I am beautiful.

I am landslide and crater shake.

I am human in all the faults that build me.
I am loved.

If this feels wrong or foreign,

that is okay.

Sail on the violence of its awkward,
court it as your new addiction
And breathe.

- Denise Jolly

IF YOU LOVE WE WILL BE SHELTER, WE WILL BE SHELTER LOVES . . .

Our Poison Horse
by Derrick Brown

Pansy
by Andrea Gibson

Courage: Daring Poems for Gutsy Girls
edited by Karen Finneyfrock, Mindy Nettifee & Rachel McKibbens

The Smell of Good Mud
by Lauren Zuniga

The Year of No Mistakes
by Cristin O'Keefe Aptowicz

Write Bloody Publishing distributes and promotes great books of fiction, poetry, and art every year. We are an independent press dedicated to quality literature and book design, with an office in Austin, TX.

Our employees are authors and artists, so we call ourselves a family. Our design team comes from all over America: modern painters, photographers, and rock album designers create book covers we're proud to be judged by.

We publish and promote 8 to 12 tour-savvy authors per year. We are grass-roots, D.I.Y., bootstrap believers. Pull up a good book and join the family. Support independent authors, artists, and presses.

**Want to know more about Write Bloody books, authors, and events?
Join our mailing list at**

www.writebloody.com

WRITE BLOODY BOOKS

CPSIA information can be obtained at www.ICGtesting.com
Printed in the USA
BVOW05s2053170315

392154BV00001B/1/P